POWERSHELL SQL

****

POWERSHELL SQL

Copyright © 2019. All Rights Reserved.

DISCLAIMER

The information contained within this eBook is strictly for educational purposes. If you wish to apply ideas contained in this eBook, you are taking full responsibility for your actions.

The author has made every effort to ensure the accuracy of the information within this book was correct at time of publication. The author does not assume and hereby disclaims any liability to any party for any loss, damage, or disruption caused by errors or omissions, whether such errors or omissions result from accident, negligence, or any other cause.

WHY YOU SHOULD READ THIS BOOK

SQL stands for Structured Query Language and is a declarative programming language for accessing and editing data in RDBMS (Relational Database Management Systems). SQL was developed by IBM in the 1970s for the mainframe platform. Several years later, SQL was standardized by both the American National Standards Institute (ANSI-SQL) and the International Organization for Standardization (ISO-SQL). According to ANSI, SQL is pronounced "es queue el", but many software and database developers with background knowledge in MS SQL Server pronounce it to be "continued".

What is RDBMS?

A relational database management system is software that is used to store and manage data in database objects called tables. A relational database table is a tabular data structure arranged in columns and rows. The table columns, also known as table fields, have unique names and different attributes that define the column type, default value, indexes, and various other column characteristics. The rows of the relational database table are the actual data entries.

Most popular SQL RDBMS

The most popular RDBMS are MS SQL Server from Microsoft, Oracle from Oracle Corp., DB2 from IBM, MySQL from MySQL and MS Access from Microsoft. Most commercial database vendors have developed their proprietary SQL extension based on the ANSI SQL standard. For example, the SQL version used by MS SQL Server is called Transact-SQL or simply T-SQL. The Oracle version is called PL / SQL (short for Procedural Language / SQL), and MS Access uses Jet-SQL.

What can you do with SQL?

o SQL queries are used to retrieve data from database tables. The SQL queries use the SELECT SQL keyword that is part of the Data Query Language (DQL). If we have a table called "Orders" and you want to select all the items whose order value is greater than $ 100, you can do so with the following SQL SELECT query:

- SELECT OrderID, ProductID, CustomerID, OrderDate, OrderValue

- FROM orders

- WHERE Order value> 200

- ORDER BY OrderValue;

POWERSHELL SQL

The FROM SQL clause specifies which table (s) of data is being retrieved. The WHERE SQL clause specifies search criteria (in our case, to retrieve only records with an order value greater than $ 200). The ORDER BY clause indicates that the returned data must be sorted by the OrderValue column. The clauses WHERE and ORDER BY are optional.

> ➤ You can edit data stored in relational database tables using the SQL INSERT, UPDATE, and DELETE keywords. These three SQL commands are part of the Data Manipulation Language (DML).

- To insert data into a table named Orders, you can use an SQL statement that resembles the following:

POWERSHELL SQL

- INSERT INTO orders (ProductID, CustomerID, OrderDate, OrderValue)

VALUES (10, 108, '12 / 12/2007 ', 99.95);

- To change data in a table, you can use a statement like the following:

  ✓ UPDATE orders
  ✓ SET OrderValue = 199.99

WHERE CustomerID = 10 AND OrderDate = '12 / 12/2007 ';

- To delete data from the database table, use a statement like the following:

- ✓ Delete orders
- ✓ WHERE CustomerID = 10;

> You can create, modify, or delete database objects (examples of database objects are database tables, views, stored procedures, and so on) using the CREATE, ALTER, and DROP SQL keywords. These three SQL keywords are part of the Data Definition Language (DDL). For example, to create the Orders table, you can use the following SQL statement:

CREATE orders

(Order ID INT IDENTITY (1, 1) PRIMARY KEY, ProductID INT, Customer number, OrderDate DATE, Order value currency)

> ➢ You can control permissions on database objects using the GRANT and REVOKE keywords, which are part of the Data Control Language (DCL). For example, to allow the user with user name "User1" to select data from the Orders table, you can use the following SQL statement:

GRANT SELECT ON Orders to User1

Why SQL?

Today, every software professional needs at least a basic understanding of how SQL works. If you are new to SQL, you may feel overwhelmed and confused at first. As you progress, however, you'll see how powerful and elegant SQL is.

Table of Contents

DISCLAIMER...3

WHY YOU SHOULD READ THIS BOOK.................4

INTRODUCTION..15

CHAPTER 1 20

   HISTORY OF MICROSOFT SQL SERVER 20

CHAPTER 2 23

   WHAT IS SQL AND WHY IT IS IMPORTANT?.23

CHAPTER 3 27

   WHEN SHOULD YOU USE MICROSOFT SQL
   SERVER OVER MICROSOFT ACCESS?............27

CHAPTER 4 35

   SHOULD YOU PAY A HOSTING COMPANY TO
   HOST MICROSOFT LYNC? 35

      COMPLETE DETAILS ABOUT MICROSOFT
      SHAREPOINT 2010 CONFIGURING
      CERTIFICATION..38

      REASONS TO CONSIDER UPGRADING TO
      WINDOWS SERVER 2012..........................42

      GETTING STARTED WITH EXCHANGE 2010
     53

CHAPTER 5 75

POWERSHELL SQL

HARDENING YOUR WEB APPLICATION
AGAINST SQL INJECTIONS 75

CHAPTER 6 86

DO A 'SKILL AUDIT' AT YOUR WORKPLACE - IT
COULD BENEFIT YOU A LOT 86

CHAPTER 7 90

WHAT IS SQL INJECTION 90

CHAPTER 8 101

SQL FROM NOTHING TO SOMETHING - A
HANDS-ON BEGINNING TUTORIAL USING SQL
SERVER EXPRESS EDITION 101

CHAPTER 9 108

MICROSOFT SQL AZURE - MICROSOFT TAKES
SQL DATABASES TO THE CLOUDS 108

CHAPTER 10 116

HOW TO RESTORE SQL DATABASE EASILY
WITHOUT ANY DIFFICULTY? 116

CHAPTER 11 122

THE INS AND OUTS OF SQL INJECTION 122

CHAPTER 12 137

IBM ISERIES AS/400 SQL PERFORMANCE .. 137

CHAPTER 13 148

MICROSOFT ACCESS TO SQL SERVER
MIGRATION 148

CHAPTER 14 157

STUDYING FOR 1Z0-047: ORACLE DATABASE
SQL EXPERT 157

CHAPTER 15 168

FILESTREAM CORRUPTION IN SQL - A
PHENOMENAL SQL DATABASE RECOVERY
SOLUTION! 168

CHAPTER 16 172

THE KEY FEATURES OF MICROSOFT SQL
SERVER 2005 172

CHAPTER 17 175

UNDERSTANDING SQL WEB HOSTING 175

CHAPTER 18 179

PERFECTLY NEW DATABASE QUERY TOOL -
FOXY SQL PRO RELEASED 179

CHAPTER 19 185

ORACLE SQL CERTIFICATION: 1Z0-051 OR
1Z0-061? 185

CHAPTER 20 190

STUDY GUIDE FOR 1Z0-061: ORACLE
DATABASE 12C: SQL FUNDAMENTALS........190

POWERSHELL SQL

CHAPTER 21 194

HOW TO RESET SA PASSWORD IN SQL
SERVER 2000 194

    PL-SQL INSTRUCTIONS 197

CHAPTER 22 203

VMWARE VCENTER AND MICROSOFT SQL
SERVER REPORTING SERVICES 203

CONCLUSION 206

REFERENCES 213

INTRODUCTION

Would you like to compare application software from leading vendors? Compare computer software from the software giants on the Internet. You can view comparisons by the most popular brands, alphabetically or by price range. Shop on CNet to compare computer software specs and prices side-by-side.

Visit the Internet for unbiased reviews and comparisons on the top tuneup computer software. The best brands of a given product are compared, to provide enough information to decide what is the best make, brand or model.

Unleash the full power of your PC and give your system a super performance boost with Advanced Windows Care Professional. The software is an all-in-one and automatic system maintenance with anti-spyware, privacy protection, performance tune-ups, and system cleaning features.

POWERSHELL SQL

Read the full profile on the leading computer monitoring software vendors. When comparing the software, consider four software vendors: Argent, BMC Software, NetIQ Solutions and Quest Software. Which software best suits you?

Argent is the world's leading private software company, with offices worldwide. Customers use Argent's products to enhance the performance of Java, .NET, SAP, Oracle E-Business, PeopleSoft, and Siebel and the boost the manageability and availability of databases like Oracle, SQL Server, DB2, Sybase, and MySQL.

Argent's products enhance the performance of infrastructures, including Active Directory, Migration, Windows, SharePoint, Unix, Linux, SQL Server, PowerShell, Messaging/Exchange and Group Policy Management. Argent can scale its products to meet a wide variety of applications, from the smallest to the largest network.

BMC's products are designed to enable IT to become a key business driver. In addition to automating IT, they allow companies to monitor, manage, and perform key activities, including data recovery, systems management, customer relationship service level management, data storage management, and infrastructure management tasks.

The solutions developed by this company span enterprise systems, applications, and databases. Its mainframe service management segment includes job scheduling and output management solutions, while its enterprise services management segment provides distributed system performance, and transaction management solutions.

NetIQ Solutions offers a range of products designed to enhance IT management capabilities, improve service, and reduce costs. The company's software includes performance management, security management, Windows administration, configuration management, enterprise administration, VoIP management, and change control management products.

POWERSHELL SQL

Yielding measurable business value and results that businesses require, the solutions help IT organizations deliver critical business services, mitigate operational risk, and document policy compliance. The solutions also help companies enhance process improvement activities and solve technically related issues.

Located in Aliso Viejo, CA, Quest Software develops and markets software designed to help companies solve challenging IT problems and achieve operational excellence. Quest's software helps boost the performance, reliability, availability, and manageability of databases, applications, and Windows infrastructures.

Users employ its software to monitor, manage, and control application environments, enhance the performance and manageability of databases, and deliver comprehensive management, migration, and integration capabilities. Its products also help companies meet compliance obligations, simplify and automate infrastructures, and perform security and identity management activities.

Look for consumer reviews and comparisons on the top 10 computer software applications. You will find software, such as home, lifestyle, design, multi media, business, productivity, educational, communications, and more. Comparing computer software will assist you in making an informed decision when obtaining software.

CHAPTER 1

HISTORY OF MICROSOFT SQL SERVER

Microsoft SQL training is important to IT professionals interested in knowing how to work on the product. A history of Microsoft SQL server is also very important. Basically, the code for MS SQL came from the Sybase SQL Server, which was the first database Microsoft attempted. It competed against Sybase, IBM and Oracle. Then, Sybase, Microsoft, and Ashton-Tate worked together to create the first version of the SQL Server. It ended up being pretty much the same as the third edition of the Sybase SQL Server. Then, the Microsoft SQL Server 4.2 was available in 1992. When the 4.21 version was available it was at the same time as Windows NT 3.1. The first version of SQL that did not include any assistance from Sybase was the Microsoft SQL Server v6.0.

When Windows NT made an appearance Sybase and Microsoft moved on to pursue their own interests. This allowed Microsoft to negotiate exclusive rights to the versions of SQL that were written for Microsoft systems. The Sybase server actually changed its name to Adaptive Server Enterprise to keep it from being confused with the Microsoft version. Many revisions have been made without assistance from Sybase since the two parted ways. The first database server written on GUI was a complete change from the Sybase code.

Currently, Microsoft SQL Server 2005 is the most recent version. It was launched beside the Visual Studio 2005. Free download of the SQL Server 2005 Express Edition is available, which is a nice bonus for people who need it. Since the release of SQL Server 2000 there have been many advancement and changes to the product. Performance has been improved, complementary systems are now available with the system, and client IDE tools are included. Some of the new systems included are Analysis Services,

POWERSHELL SQL

ETL, and messaging technologies like notification services and service broker.

With all the changes going on with each edition it is important for IT techs to take SQL 2005 training classes. With SQL 2005 training IT techs are better able to provide support for users running SQL 2005 as well as other versions. There are quite a few classes available online for SQL training or else classes are offered in person in boot camps, night classes, or weekend classes. You just have to find the right class for you, take it, and then you will be prepared to work on all of the SQL servers.

CHAPTER 2

WHAT IS SQL AND WHY IT IS IMPORTANT?

Network programs are now bigger and more flexible. More often than not, the basic scheme of operations are mostly a combination of scripts that handle the control of a database.

Because of the diversity of languages and existing databases, the way to "talk" between each other can often be complicated and challenging, luckily for us, the presence of standards that allow us to perform the usual procedures through a wide-spread form makes this confusing job more straightforward.

That's what Structured Query Language (SQL) is centered on, which happens to be nothing but an international standard language of communication within databases. That is why, the Structured Query Language (SQL) is truly a standardized language that allows all of us to implement any language e.g. ASP or PHP, in conjunction with any specific database e.g. MySQL, SQL Server, MS Access.

SQL was manufactured by IBM during the1970's, in the beginning it was called SEQUEL (Structure English Query Language). Years later, Microsoft and Oracle also started using SEQUEL. Their global recognition and used grew and then the term SEQUEL was changed. In 1986, the term SEQUEL was standardized by the American National Standards Institute (ANSI) to SQL. In other words, they ditched the world "English" from the term.

Until this day, there are lots of users who refuse to refer to it as SQL, to these people, SEQUEL certainly is the right name for this international standardized database language. SQL has additionally been revised in 1989 and then 1992 (SQL-92). Ever since,SQL has undergone many revisions to enhance their standardization.

SQL is surely an international standardized language, but that does not mean that is similar for each database. Believe it or not, some databases execute particular functions that will not always run in others. That's the reason why every company that delivers database products, for instance Microsoft and Oracle, have their own certification process ensuring that those that takes the certification exam are very well prepared and understand the differences between the various models of SQL. Their knowledge is focus on their own unique specific version of SQL.

SQL is not simply relevant because of the ability to standardized an otherwise confusing language, it provides two other unique characteristics. On one hand, it really is tremendously flexible and powerful. On the other hand, it is very accessible which makes it simpler to master.

There are many databases products that support SQL, however, two of the biggest and most widely used are Microsoft SQL server and Oracle database.

Each company that offers database product has their own path to become an "expert". For example, Microsoft offers a variety of certifications to ensure that every Microsoft SQL Certified meets their criteria. Oracle does the same thing with their Certification process.

CHAPTER 3

WHEN SHOULD YOU USE MICROSOFT SQL SERVER OVER MICROSOFT ACCESS?

Two of the coolest tools that have ever come out from Microsoft are certainly Microsoft SQL Server and Microsoft Access. Microsoft Access databases have certainly become more prevalent over the last 2 years as large corporations break the imposed ban on using the tool. Many of our large corporate clients and government clients have stymied development in Microsoft Access for varying reasons which can include security issues or simply the IT Managements belief that they don't want to support the application.

Some of the reasons why IT Departments do not want Microsoft Access in their environments are quite valid. For example, the use of Access Databases in high security areas such as in the Education Department for storing student information, Department of Defence systems, Hospitals storing patient data are all valid reasons why data should not be stored in a MS Access Database.

However, one of the key advantages that Microsoft Access has is the ability to build a software system to manage a range of services very quickly. The downside is that Microsoft Access on its own is very un-secure and can easily be lifted without any trace using a USB Stick or CDROM. But there are ways to secure Microsoft Access and to prevent data from being lifted.

First of all let us look at Microsoft SQL Server...

Microsoft SQL Server is the tool of choice for many corporate environments because it is a commercial database server. Its core role in the commercial world is to store data which is slightly different to Microsoft Access. MS Access whilst it is a database, it is more so a database management system that allows you to build a fully interactive user interface that allows users to enter data and report on data where as Microsoft SQL Server simply stores the data within tables. It doesn't have the ability to provide you with a front-end like ms Access.

Microsoft SQL Server allows you to store large volumes of data which include items like photographs, video, text, numbers and much much more. Now whilst I'm sure everyone is saying, "But Microsoft Access can do that too", you are right to a certain extent but Microsoft Access has very defined limits. Microsoft SQL Server is designed to handle terra bytes worth of data where as Microsoft Access can only hand around 1 Gigabyte of data without having issues.

Can You Use Microsoft SQL Server and Microsoft Access together...

The answer to this question is a resounding YES. In fact my preferred way of developing systems is to utilise MS SQL Server as the datastore and then use MS Access as the Front End. To join the two together I simply link the SQL tables to Microsoft Access via an ODBC connection.

This method is what I consider the best way to build a database system which requires a medium to high level of security and integrity. There are a number of reasons for this -

1. Microsoft SQL Server integrates security into the Microsoft Windows Active Directory Security System

2. Microsoft SQL Server can be setup to automatically back up

3. It can do incremental backups which means it can backup during the day rather than just once at night

4. Using the server with the Active Directory environment means that your

users only need to have one username and only need to logon once

5. Microsoft SQL Server databases cannot easily be duplicated or copied without the SQL Server DBA (DBA stands for Database Administrator) knowing

6. It can handle Terrabytes worth of data where as Microsoft Access is questionable over 1 Gigabyte

7. Microsoft SQL Server allows you to do some of the system processes on the server via Stored Procedures and DTS (Data Transformation Services) where as Microsoft Access requires the client to do all the processing

I am quite sure most small business owners will look at this article and say, "Well I can't afford such a system". Well let me tell you,

you can. Microsoft many years ago introduced a software package called Microsoft Small Business Server. This package includes professional tools such as Microsoft SQL Server and Microsoft Exchange and they competitively priced this package for around $1500 Australian. The key reason they did this was so that small businesses would have the ability to access professional resources at an effective and cost efficient price rather than being disadvantaged.

You can buy servers in Australia with Microsoft Small business Server for around $3000 to $4000 dollars which is far more competitive than what it was a few years ago. It also means that by having Microsoft SQL Server available, the systems they can develop can be as professional as those organisations whom have multi-million dollar budgets.

The time to use ms access on its own is really dependent on whether you need your data to be mobile. If you do and the security of the data is not important, then using Microsoft Access as the data store is appropriate. For example, the other day a company who puts together mining information on key contacts, wanted to distribute their information in database format to people who want to know who's who in the industry. In this case they developed their information in an Access database and distributed it to those who were prepared to buy it in this format. Security in their case wasn't an issue because customers were paying for it, so it was appropriate to develop the system in Microsoft Access rather than any other format that might utilise Microsoft SQL Server.

If for instance, the data you are storing is in fact sensitive or is mission critical but the data needs to be mobile. For example you might need the data for a Financial Planner or Loan Mortgage Broker then in this case your data should be stored in MSDE. MSDE is in fact a cut down version of Microsoft SQL Server and by design it is far more secure than Microsoft Access plus it is much harder to copy the data.

The bottom line is this, if your data is important to your business then your principle data store should not be MS Access, you should be developing a system where your data is stored in Microsoft SQL Server and then using MS Access as the Front-End to manipulate the data. Further to this, you should be integrating your SQL Server logins with your Active Directory Security System. If you use this technique your data will be far more secure than if it is stored in Microsoft Access Exclusively.

CHAPTER 4

SHOULD YOU PAY A HOSTING COMPANY TO HOST MICROSOFT LYNC?

Lync 2010 is Microsoft's latest instant messaging, presence, and collaboration suite for PC, smart phone, and Internet. It creates a real-world communications experience over a network with streaming high-resolution video and audio. This chapter will focus on the benefits of having a hosting company run and support Lync in a cloud based virtual network. Why pay a hosting company for Lync when you could purchase, install, and run it yourself?

First off, Lync has a hefty set of hardware system requirements. Businesses that already outsource their networking needs are not likely to have a system that is capable of running Lync without significant investment and upgrades. And those with in-house networks are not likely to have a Lync compatible platform either. Recommended server requirements to run Lync include a 64-bit dual or quad processor, quad-core, 2.0 GHz or higher (Intel Itanium processors are not supported for Lync Server 2010), at least 16 GB of memory, and local storage with at least 72 GB free disk space on a 10,000 RPM disk drive. In addition, at least 1 network adapter is required (2 recommended), each 1 Gbps or higher. A cloud hosting company can meet these hardware requirements with a much lower monthly service fee.

Software requirements are also significant. Lync 2010 is available only in 64-bit, which requires 64-bit hardware and 64-bit editions of Windows Server. Lync is not available in a 32-bit version. Computers running Lync Server administrative tools must run a 64-bit edition Windows 7 or Vista operating system. Database management systems for the back-end database, the Archiving database, and the Monitoring database require a 64-bit edition of Microsoft SQL Server 2008 as well. Additional software requirements include Windows PowerShell 2.0 and.NET Framework 3.5 with SP1.

Lync requires a specialized technical staff to install, backup, and maintain it. An IT staff with the skills and experience to run Lync is going to be expensive. A cloud hosting company can provide this specialized support without the overhead. Select cloud hosts also offer a 100% up time guarantee, with a 24-hour support staff running redundant clusters and multiple connections, with full-data backup in case of a system crash. And if your company already has an active directory, a cloud host staff can integrate it with Lync for a seamless transition.

Another benefit of having a hosting company run Lync is scalability. Your Lync network can grow with your company without expensive hardware and software purchases and upgrades. And at any time, if you need to scale back, you can. Security issues associated with network based communications are covered as well. Physical and virtual firewalls, anti-virus, and secured connections are included as part of most cloud hosting network services.

To put it simply, a cloud host can save you significant time and money. A host would make expensive hardware and software purchases and upgrades unnecessary, and provide an IT support staff to run and maintain it all for a low monthly fee. Lync could infinitely scale with your business, and you could scale back at any time if needed. And finally, your network communications would be safe and secure with redundant physical and virtual security features.

COMPLETE DETAILS ABOUT MICROSOFT SHAREPOINT 2010 CONFIGURING CERTIFICATION

Exam 70-667 is one of the hottest certifications from Microsoft and the examination name is Microsoft SharePoint 2010 configuring. This certification course is designed for the IT professionals who are responsible in handling Microsoft SharePoint 2010 application. The certification validates the candidate's knowledge and skills on the ability to manage and administer the Microsoft SharePoint 2010 application installation.

Eligibility Criteria:

The minimum eligibility criteria to apply for 70-667 examination are as follows:

- Candidates should have considerable working experience in administering, installing, and configuring

- Candidates should have at least 6 months working experience in deploying and managing the SharePoint solutions and architectures

- Candidates should be proficient in Microsoft SQL 2005 or higher level server,

POWERSHELL SQL

DNS, IIS 7.0, and active directory relating to SharePoint

- Candidates should be proficient in Windows 2008 server security and infrastructure

- Candidates should have considerable working experience in IT business operations including restore, back-up and high availability

- Candidates should also have considerable working experience in command line administration and Windows PowerShell version 2

If a candidate has all the above mentioned requirements, then the candidate can register this examination in any of the nearby Pearson VUE or Promotric centers. Registration is also possible through online but necessary proofs have to be submitted for verification purposes. After verification is done, candidate will receive an email regarding the status. If the application is approved, candidate can pay the fee and schedule for the exam at any time.

Course Blueprint:

The following are the course blueprint and percentage of questions from each topic:

- SharePoint environment installation and configuration- 25% questions

- SharePoint environment managing- 26% questions

- SharePoint environment deploying and managing- 24% questions

- SharePoint environment maintenance- 25% questions

REASONS TO CONSIDER UPGRADING TO WINDOWS SERVER 2012

So Microsoft bounces in with another brand new server product. Generally, we find new versions of Microsoft server products are better than their predecessors and certainly much better than their desktop operating system counterparts which have caused a few ripples of excitement but more of nervousness and people seem to be awaiting the inevitable service pack 1 release.

Having had a play with the release preview of Windows Server 2012, we have discovered some interesting things about the new server to share with you. Some people are sceptical about the new interface formerly known as Metro, but with more emphasis on Server Core and the Minimal Server Interface, the UI is unlikely to be the deciding factor when choosing to upgrade. More important are the big changes and new capabilities that make Server 2012 better able to handle your network's workloads and needs.

Here are 11 reasons to give serious consideration to upgrading to Server 2012 sooner rather than later.

1: Freedom of interface choice

A Server Core installation provides security and performance advantages, but in the past, you had to make a choice: If you installed Server Core, you were stuck with it with only the command line as your interface. However, this changes with Windows Server 2012.

Microsoft realised that the command line is great for some tasks and the graphical interface is preferable for others. Server 2012 makes the GUI a "feature" - one that can be turned on and off at will, therefore saving resources when the server is simply being a server. You do it through the Remove Roles or Features option in Server Manager.

2: Server Manager

Regarding the Server Manager, even many of those who dislike the new (metro) tile-based interface overall have admitted that the design's implementation in the new Server Manager is brilliant.

One of the best things about the new Server Manager is the multi-server capabilities, which makes it easy to deploy roles and features remotely to physical and virtual servers. It's easy to create a server group - a collection of servers that can be managed together. The remote administration improvements let you provision servers without having to make an RDP connection.

3: Server Message Block 3.0

The SMB protocol has been significantly improved in Windows Server 2012 as well as Windows 8. The new version supports new file server features, like SMB transparent failover, SMB Scale Out, SMB Multichannel, SMB Direct, SMB encryption, VSS for SMB file sharing, SMB directory leasing, and SMB PowerShell. It also works beautifully with Hyper-V, so that VHD files and virtual machine configuration files can be hosted on SMB 3.0 shares. A SQL system database can be stored on an SMB share, as well, with improvements to performance.

4: Dynamic Access Control (DAC)

Microsoft has shifted the focus from separate security products to a more "baked in" approach of integrating security into every part of the operating system.

Dynamic Access Control is one such example, helping IT Pros create more centralized security models for access to network resources by tagging sensitive data both manually and automatically, based on factors such as the file content or the creator. After that, claims based access controls can be applied.

5: Storage Spaces

Storage is an interesting topic in the IT industry these days. We are still a long way off storing everything in the cloud many organizations are still concerned about security and reliability. There are a myriad of solutions for storing data on your network in a way that provides better utilisation of storage resources, centralized management, better scalability along with security and reliability, SANs and NAS do that, but they can be expensive.

Storage Spaces is a fantastic new feature in Server 2012 that lets you use inexpensive hard drives to create a storage pool, which can then be divided into spaces that are used like physical disks. They can include hot standby drives and use redundancy methods such as 2- or 3-way mirroring or parity. What's great is that you can add new disks any time, and a space can be larger than the physical capacity of the pool. When you add new drives, the space automatically uses the extra capacity.

6: Virtualisation

Virtualisation was the biggest thing before the cloud hit the IT industry and it is still the thing to do when it comes to servers. Hyper-V is Microsoft's answer to VMware / XenServer. Microsoft's virtualisation platform is liked by a lot of IT Pro's and with each new version Windows hypervisor gets a little better, and Hyper-V in Windows Server 2012 brings a number of new features to the table. One of the most interesting is Hyper-V Replica.

This is a replication mechanism that will be a disaster recovery Godsend to SMBs that may not be able to deploy complex and costly replication solutions. It logs changes to the disks in a VM and uses compression to save on bandwidth, replicating from a primary server to a replica server.

You are able to store multiple snapshots of a VM on the replica server and then select the one you want to use. It works with both standalone hosts and clusters in any combination.

7: Virtual Desktop Infrastructure

Windows Terminal Services was renamed Remote Desktop Services and has since expanded to encompass much more than the ability to RDP into the desktop of a remote server. Microsoft then launched a centralized Virtual Desktop Infrastructure

(VDI) solution in Windows Server 2008 R2 and now some significant improvements have been made in Server 2012.

You no longer need a dedicated GPU graphics card in the server to use RemoteFX, which vastly improves the quality of graphics over RDP. Instead, you can use a virtualised GPU on standard server hardware. USB over RDP is much better, and the Fair Share feature can manage how CPU, memory, disk space, and bandwidth are allocated among users to stop certain users stealing all the bandwidth.

8: DirectAccess

DirectAccess was supposed to be Microsoft's "VPN replacement" It allowed you to create a secure connection from client to corporate network without the performance drain and with a more transparent user experience than a traditional VPN. Administrators get more control over the machines and the ability to manage them even before users log in. Group policy is utilised to control the machines as well and there is no hassle of setting up a VPN connection.

So why hasn't Direct Access taken off? Two main reasons, it can't be virtualised and its dependent on IPv6. However in Windows Server 2012, DirectAccess now works with IPv4 and lo and behold it can run on a Hyper-V virtual machine. It also comes with a new wizard to help make configuration a lot easier.

9: Resilient File System

NTFS has been around since 1993 and it's been a long and well needed replacement for a while. There was speculation early on that a new file system would be introduced with Windows 7, but it didn't materialise.

Windows Server 2012 finally brings us our long-awaited new file system, the Resilient File System. While it supports many of the NTFS features, a few have been abandoned, i.e. file compression, EFS, and disk quotas. However, instead we get data verification, auto correction and it's designed to work with Storage Spaces to create shrinkable/expandable logical storage pools.

Maximum scalability is the key drive behind ReFS, supporting up to 16 exabytes in practice. ReFS supports a theoretical limit of 256 zetabytes (more than 270 billion terabytes) that allows for a lot of scaling and a whole bunch of cloud storage!

10: Easy licensing

Microsoft and easy licencing don't really go in the same sentence. However Microsoft have actually listened this time and Windows Server 2012 is offered in only four editions: Datacenter, Standard, Essentials and Foundation. The first two are licensed per-processor plus CAL and the other two (for small businesses) are licensed per-server with limits on the number of user accounts (15 for Foundation and 25 for Essentials)

11: The New Active Directory

In today's business environments, data is not always stored on the customer's server due to the utilisation of cloud technology. In addition data is accessed by staff on various different devices like phones, laptops, desktops and other removable devices.

To address these new challenges, organizations have to change how they approach identity and security. Windows Server 2012 contribution to helping with this challenge is the introduction of Dynamic Access Control, and it brings with it exciting new capabilities and deployment options for Direct Access. This means you will be able to better manage and protect data access, simplify deployment and management of your identity infrastructure and provide more secure access to data from virtually anywhere.

GETTING STARTED WITH EXCHANGE 2010

As most know Exchange 2010 is the latest version of Microsoft's email server. I wanted to write a short description of the software and outline its features.

Like its predecessor Exchange 2010 requires that you run it on an x64 platform. 32-bit processing is surely but slowly becoming a thing of the past. In 2010 however you must also be running Windows 2008 SP2 or 2008 R2. One of the major decisions you'll have to make is whether to select the standard or enterprise edition. This basically boils down to how many stores you need. Standard supports 5 stores per server as to where Enterprise you can do 50+. As far as the client side CAL's are concerned you must purchase the 2008 enterprise CAL's if you wish to do unified messaging. There is not however a limitation in the software. It is simply a licensing issue. Which means you'll still have the ability to access unified messaging but it will not be licensed correctly. Another feature Microsoft has decided to keep is the JET EDB database. It has been rumored in the past that Microsoft would start using SQL server to house the Exchange database. This is not the case.

If you ever worked with recovery storage groups in Exchange 2003 or 2007 you will no longer find those in 2010. As well you will not be able to find routing groups. All of the Exchange 2010's routing is done through active directory sites and services. So you must make sure that you have properly configured your sites before moving forward with Exchange. It is essential to Exchange 2010 functioning properly. As with Exchange 2007 Microsoft still is trying to de-emphasize public folders. Their goal is to eventually replace these with their Sharepoint product.

Another major feature of Exchange 2007 and 2010 is their ability to reject email at the gateway. The Edge transport server allows you to configure ADAM and active directory lightweight services to query AD. This allows you to get a list of valid email address and push them out to the border of your network. If the edge server detects that someone is trying to send email to the inside of your organization and the user does not exist it is dropped immediately. This saves on memory and processing power internally so that you don't have to deal with spam.

Additionally with Exchange 2007 and 2010 you get the ability to create UNC direct file access paths. This way in OWA when a user needs a file on a network share they can grab it without needing a cumbersome VPN client. Outlook anywhere also remains widely the same in 2007 and 2010. It basically encapsulates your RPC packets into https packets. This allows you to traverse your firewall without opening any additional ports. Therefore giving users access to their email from Outlook wherever they may travel.

One of the greatest new features of Exchange 2010 in my opinion is database availability groups or DAG. This is essentially the same thing as CCR in Exchange 2007. Anyone who has tried to configure CCR, LCR, or SCR in Exchange 2007 knows that it can be quite the process. Microsoft simplified this with DAG's in 2010. It allows you to keep 16 copies of a users mailbox for redundancy and disaster recovery. It does this through a process called log shipping. Where 1MB files are created and then played into the database. This allows you to keep a backup of your server at another physical location for disaster recovery or have two Exchange servers running next to each other.

Another nice feature in 2010 is the fact that the client access server or CAS redirects your client to their database server that houses their mailbox. You no longer need to specify the location of your server in Outlook. The CAS parses AD and redirects them automatically. Therefore there is no hard coding. This makes the transition for fail over a lot easier.

As most of you know who have used Exchange 2007 the GUI is simply a front end to Microsofts command line utility called EMS or Exchange Mangement Shell. Anything you do in the GUI is converted to a command and executed against your server. I would personally say you have about 90 percent functionality in the GUI as opposed to EMS. However, EMS definitely makes the process a lot easier if you need to apply a setting to multiple objects at the same time.

As with Exchange 2007 you still have the same five roles edge transport, hub transport, client access server, mailbox, and unified messaging. Inside of these five roles only the edge transport server must be installed separately from the rest of the servers. Everything else can be ran on one box. Although this is not recommend for performance reasons. The reason why the edge server is standalone is it was meant to sit in your DMZ or on the border of your network. Absorbing the hits so your internal servers are not affected. It has features such as safelist aggregation where Outlook client rules are brought outside to it so that it can apply those rules before the message ever enters your internal network.

The hub server still is the same as Exchange 2007 it routes your messages internally and holds compliance rules. You can also run a command against it to install antispam feature set. This way if you don't have an edge transport server you can use it to receive outside mail directly. Although this is not recommended by Microsoft.

POWERSHELL SQL

The CAS server or client access server is meant to interface with your internal and external clients. As stated before it automatically redirects your Outlook clients so that you don't need to hardcode their mailbox server. It also accepts connections from smart phones, OWA, etc. It is basically your clients interface to your Exchange infrastructure.

If you wish to monitor your Exchange 2010 infrastructure Microsoft has made a plugin for their SCOM or system center operations manager. This is Microsoft's MOM replacement that allows you to monitor your servers.

In Exchange 2010 you will no longer see SCR, LCR, or CCR. They have been superseded by DAG or database availability groups. This makes configuring database replication a lot smoother. DAG's also allow for your data to reside across multiple servers. You can also have multiple DAG's.

This is a great feature because if half of your users are in one DAG group and it goes down the other half are not even affected. Other benefits are reduced restore time since you're not restoring all of your users' data only the ones in that DAG. You can also have separate exchange policies for different DAG's. So if your management is in one and your regular users are in another you can change the rules that apply to them. This is a great way to mitigate risk by distributing your load.

As far as the enterprise and standard software go they are both installed from the same media. It is just different license keys that you input that determine what version you are installing. It is also upgradable. You can go from trial to standard to enterprise. However, you cannot downgrade backwards from enterprise to standard or standard to trial.

In order to install Exchange 2010 your domain and forest functional level must be at 2003. Also each site which contains Exchange 2010 must also contain a 2003SP2 domain controller or 2008 domain controller. We recommend you have your domain running 2008R2 domain controllers however.

Exchange still uses EAS or exchange active sync for mobile devices. This way your contacts, calendar, email, etc. are all tightly integrated with your Windows mobile devices.

One common misconception that people have is Exchange enterprise must be installed on server enterprise software. Or that server enterprise software cannot have Exchange standard installed on it. Both of these are fallacies.

POWERSHELL SQL

When you begin your Exchange installation you should give serious consideration to how you configure your arrays. Exchange is a very read/write intensive application. Therefore you should separate your OS, log files, and database all on separate arrays. If this is not possible it is then recommended that you at least put yoru OS and log files on one array and your database files on another. The reason for this is simple. The log files are write intensive and the database files are read intensive. Separate these two out can speed up your disk I/O.

Memory requirements in Exchange 2010 have pretty much gone unchanged. Start your server with 2GB of memory and then 5MB for every mailbox user. I would also personally recommend to have a minimum of 4GB. Memory is cheap enough these days that the benefit of having more of it out way the cost.

POWERSHELL SQL

Although the databases in Exchange can grow very large we do not recommend that you go over 100GB. This can become cumbersome to work with and decrease performance on your server.

If you wish to remotely manage your Exchange server you can install the management tools. They will install on Vista SP2 and higher or server 2008 SP2 or higher. This way you do not have to remotely login to your Exchange server to make all of your changes.

As far as your site layout goes you should also plan on having a global catalog server in every location that contains a mailbox server. This is recommended by Microsoft and will reduce WAN traffic.

Exchange has also setup a new permissions setup which they refer to as RBAC or role based access control. From this you get 5 roles to manage your exchange infrastructure. They are Organization management, view only organization management, recipient management, records management, and GAL synchronization management.

Another thing you should consider before installing Exchange 2010 is to make sure your domain is setup properly. You can use tools such as NETDIAG and DCDIAG to verify this. In order to install Exchange 2010 you're going to need to be a member of domain admins, enterprise admins, and schema admins. You will also want to add connect Microsoft.com and download.microsoft.com to your trusted sites list in IE. Other pieces of software that must be installed are.NET 3.5, Windows remote management 2.0, powershell v2, 2007 office converter Microsoft filter packs. If you are installing the mailbox role you must also have AD services remote management tools.

POWERSHELL SQL

Before starting the install you must prepare
your schema by running setup /ps if it fails
delete the contents of c:windowstemp, copy
the files from your CD to your hard drive
and rerun setup /ps. You must then run setup
/prepareAD
/OrganizationName:MyCompany   where
"MyCompany" can be replaced by your
organization name.

You must then prepare the prerequisites by
running the following commands.

ServerManagerCMD -install RSAT-ADDS
ServerManagerCMD -install Web-Server
ServerManagerCMD -install Web-ISAPI-
Ext ServerManagerCMD -install Web-
Metabase ServerManagerCMD -install
Web-Lgcy-Mgmt-Console
ServerManagerCMD -install Web-Basic-
Auth ServerManagerCMD -install Web-
Digest-Auth ServerManagerCMD -install
Web-Windows-Auth ServerManagerCMD -
install   Web-Dyn-Compression

POWERSHELL SQL

ServerManagerCMD -install Net-http-Activation ServerManagerCMD -install RPC-over-http-Proxy Once this is complete reboot your server. You are now ready to run Setup.com /mode:install /roles:H,C,M the H,C,M install hub cas and mailbox roles.

Once your install is complete run the Exchange BPA or best practice analyzer.

In order to install the Edge server you'll want to make sure you're running 2008 standard with SP2. You'll need.NET 3.5, remote management 2.0, powershell v2, AD LDS (can be installed via servermanagerCMD -i ADLDS). For the edge server to work in a DMZ you'll need to open ports 50389-50636. Then run new-EdgeSubscription -filename "c:tempEdgeSubscriptionInfo.xml" Copy that generated file to your hub server you can import it in the GUI and run start-edgeSubscription from EMS. You can test this once it is imported to verify it is working properly by using test-EdgeSubscription from EMS.

I would personally recommend using a RBL provider to stop spam from entering your organization. One example of this is SpamHaus. This queries the connecting server to a black list of IP's and blocks communication if it is found on the list. This one feature can drastically cut down on spam.

Another item you have to address is purchasing a SAN certificate for your Exchange server. Exchange has moved to a secure by default mentality. You will find connecting to OWA or using active sync become very painful if you try to issue your own SSL certificates.

Another security improvement in Exchange 2007 and 2010 is that all intercommunication is secure and encrypted.

POWERSHELL SQL

TLS is used for all server to server communication internally. RPC is used for your Outlook clients to communicate with your servers. SSL is configured for all external client communication including, OWA, activesync, etc.

Opportunistic TLS is a new feature where your Exchange server will no long try to send via SMTP by default. It will first send a STARTTLS command to use TLS to encrypt external SMTP communication with other servers. If the other server however does not support this it will revert to insecure communications.

Still included in Exchange 2010 is the ability to use a journaling mailbox to track all of your emails. This is required by some organizations. Keep in mind that this feature can increase your processor and memory usage by 25 percent. So you should make sure your server has plenty of resources before turning on this feature.

One of the requirements as previously stated is that Exchange 2010 must be running active directory 2003. Even though 2008 is recommended if you are running Cisco Unified Messaging 4.2(1) or lower it is NOT compatible with active directory 2008.

When you upgrade your active directory infrastructure it is recommended that you create a virtual machine using Microsoft Hyper-v or Vmware. Make the virtual machine an additional domain controller and make it a global catalog. This way if your upgrade takes turn for the worst you have data that is intact if you have to downgrade. Do not forget to unplug it from the network before doing the upgrade. If you need to revert back you can use NTDSUTIL to seize the roles.

If for whatever reason you need to create a scratch installation of a domain you can always use the ADMT utility to move users, groups, computers, service accounts, and trusts.

POWERSHELL SQL

To migrate from 2003 Exchange to 2010 the overview is as follows. First you must be running Exchange 2003 with service pack 2. Your active directory domain and forest functional levels must be 2003 and at least one global catalog has to be 2003 server with SP2. Instal AD LDIFDE tools on 2008 to upgrade your schema. Upgrade your Exchange Schema. Transfer OWA, activesync, and Outlook anywhere to the CAS server. Install/upgrade hub server. Transfer the mail flow to the hub transport server. Install mailbox servers and DAG if required. Move your public folder replicas using pfmigrat.wsf or PFRecursive.PS1. Move your mailboxes. Rehome OAB. Rehome public folder hierarchy. Transfer public folder replicas. Delete 2003 public and private stores. Delete routing group connectors. Delete RUS using ADSIEdit. Uninstall Exchange 2003.

To migrate from 2007 Exchange to 2010 the process is a little less. Make sure your Exchange 2007 server is running SP2. Make sure your domain and forest is at 2003 functional level. Global catalog server is at 2003 SP2. Use AD LDIFDE tools to upgrade your schema. Prepare schema. CAS server. Transfer OWA. Install hub transport. Transfer mail to hub transport. Use AddReplicatoPFRecursive.Ps1 to move your public folder replications. Move your mailboxes. Rehome OAB. Transfer public folder replica. Delete public and private stores. Uninstall Exchange 2007.

With Exchange 2010 or 2007 you want to make your co-existence time as small as possible. The longer you intermingle different versions the more problems you are asking for.

If you are running Exchange 5.5 unfortunately there is no direct upgrade at this point. You must first upgrade to Exchange 2003 SP2 then to 2010. As far as Lotus Notes, Novell Groupwise, or Senmail goes the recommend path is to install a clean environment and then work on importing your data using tools. There is no upgrade path.

Database Availability Groups or DAG's are a very important new feature of Exchange 2010. It gives you the ability to maintain 16 copies of users' mailboxes. You can also set different databases to fail over to different servers and specify in what priority. The requirements for DAG are Windows Server 2008 enterprise, two nics in your mailboxes servers, Exchange 2010 Enterprise, a file share witness. We recommend you put this on your hub transport server. But technically it can be on any file server. It is very easy to setup as you create a share and then Exchange manages and handles the permissions.

Steps to create a DAG, Add members, and verify the DAG

POWERSHELL SQL

- ✓ New-DatabaseAvailabilityGroup -Name ExchangeDAG -WitnessServer ExchangeHT -WitnessDirectory "c:FSW" -DatabaseAvailabilityGroupIPAddresses 172.16.4.5 --Verbose
- ✓ Add-DatabaseAvailabilityGroupServer -Identity ExchangeDAG -MailboxServer ExchangeMB -Verbose
- ✓ Add-DatabaseAvailabilityGroupServer -Identity ExchangeDAG -MailboxServer ExchangeMB2 -Verbose
- ✓ Get-DatabaseAvailabilityGroup -Identity ExchangeDAG -Status

To see your network settings run

Get-DatabaseAvailabilityGroupNetwork -identity ExchangeDAG

POWERSHELL SQL

We can then add database copies by doing the following

- ✓ Add-MailboxDatabaseCopy -Identity ExchangeMB -MailboxServer ExchangeMB2
- ✓ Then check the status
- ✓ Get-MailboxDatabaseCopyStatus
- ✓ To test the health
- ✓ Test-ReplicationHealth

CHAPTER 5

HARDENING YOUR WEB APPLICATION AGAINST SQL INJECTIONS

Structured Query Language (SQL) is a specialized programming language for sending queries to databases. Most small and industrial- strength database applications can be accessed using SQL statements. SQL is both an ANSI and an ISO standard. However, many database products supporting SQL do so with proprietary extensions to the standard language. Web applications may use user-supplied input to create custom SQL statements for dynamic web page requests.

What is SQL Injection?

SQL injection is a technique that exploits a security vulnerability occurring in the database layer of a web application. The vulnerability is present when user input is either incorrectly filtered for string literal escape characters embedded in SQL statements or user input is not strongly typed and thereby unexpectedly executed. It is in fact an instance of a more general class of vulnerabilities that can occur whenever one programming or scripting language is embedded inside another.

"SQL Injection" is subset of the unverified/unsanitized user input vulnerability ("buffer overflows" are a different subset), and the idea is to convince the application to run SQL code that was not intended. If the application is creating SQL strings naively on the fly and then running them, it's straightforward to create some real surprises.

Many organization's web servers has been compromised just because of SQL Injections, including big names which I would not like to mention here, you can search it easily on Internet.

What is Blind SQL Injection?

This particular type of attack is called a blind SQL injection attack, because the attacker cannot take advantage of detailed error messages from the server or other sources of information about the application. Getting the SQL syntax right is usually the trickiest part of the blind SQL injection process and may require a lot of trial and error. But, by adding more conditions to the SQL statement and evaluating the Web application's output, an attacker will eventually determine whether the application is vulnerable to SQL injection.

Blind SQL injection a special case that plays on the web developers or website owners sense of security. While they may think that everything on the server is tightly guarded a Blind SQL injection attack will silently be playing truth or consequences with the web server. This type of attack though very time consuming is one that provides the most potentially damaging security hole. This is because an attacker gets not only access but is provided with an enormous amount of knowledge about the database and can potentially gain access to a servers file system. This type of attack is one that is automated and requires good amount of setup to succeed. But once it is done it does not require a great deal of effort to repeat.

What is Error message SQL Injection?

Web applications commonly use SQL queries with client-supplied input in the WHERE clause to retrieve data from a database. When a Web application executes such queries without validating or scanning the user-supplied data to ensure it's not harmful, a SQL injection attack can occur. By sending unexpected data, an attacker can generate and submit SQL queries to a web applications database. A test for SQL injection vulnerabilities takes place by sending the application data that generates an invalid SQL query. If the server returns an error message, that information can be used to try to gain uncontrolled access to the database. This is the basis of one of the most popular SQL injection attacks.

Hiding error messages does not stop the SQL injection attack. What typically happens is the attacker will use the knowledge gained from the failure of this attack to change tactics. What they turn to is blind SQL injection.

Why SQL Injection?

When a web application fails to properly sanitize user-supplied input, it is possible for an attacker to alter the construction of backend SQL statements. When an attacker is able to modify a SQL statement, the process will run with the same permissions as the component that executed the command. (E.g. Database server, Web application server, Web server, etc.). The impact of this attack can allow attackers to gain total control of the database or even execute commands on the system.

When a machine has only port 80 opened, your most trusted vulnerability scanner cannot return anything useful, and you know that the admin always patch his server, this is the point where malicious hacker would turn to web hacking. SQL injection is one of type of web hacking that require nothing but port 80 and it might just work even if the admin is patch-happy. It attacks on the web application (like ASP, JSP, PHP, CGI, etc) itself rather than on the web server or services running in the OS.

Types of SQL Injections:

There are four main categories of SQL Injection attacks against databases layer in Web Application

POWERSHELL SQL

1. SQL Manipulation: manipulation is process of modifying the SQL statements by using various operations such as UNION .Another way for implementing SQL Injection using SQL Manipulation method is by changing the where clause of the SQL statement to get different results.

2. Code Injection: Code injection is process of inserting new SQL statements or database commands into the vulnerable SQL statement. One of the code injection attacks is to append a SQL Server EXECUTE command to the vulnerable SQL statement. This type of attack is only possible when multiple SQL statements per database request are supported.

3. Function Call Injection: Function call injection is process of inserting various database function calls into a vulnerable SQL statement. These function calls could be making operating system calls or manipulate data in the database.

4. Buffer Overflows: Buffer overflow is caused by using function call injection. For most of the commercial and open source databases, patches are available. This type of attack is possible when the server is un-patched

SQL Injection Prevention Techniques:

Mitigation of SQL injection vulnerability would be taking one of the two paths i.e. either using stored procedures along with callable statements or using prepared statements with dynamic SQL commands. Whichever way is adopted the data validation is must.

a. Input validation

Data sanitization is key. Best way to sanitize data is to use default deny, regular expression. Write specific filters. As far as possible use numbers, numbers and letters. If there is a need to include punctuation marks of any kind, convert them by HTML encoding them. SO that " become """ or > becomes ">" For instance if the user is submitting the E-mail address allow only @, -, . And _ in addition to numbers and letters to be used and only after they have been converted to their HTML substitutes

b. Use of prepared statement

The prepared statements should be used when the stored procedures cannot be used for whatever reason and dynamic SQL commands have to be used.

Use a Prepared Statement to send precompiled SQL statements with one or more parameters. Parameter place holders in a prepared statement are represented by the? And are called bind variables. Prepared statement are generally immune to SQL Injection attacks as the database will use the value of the bind variable exclusively and not interpret the contents of the variable in any way. PL/SQL and JDBC allow for prepared statements. Prepared statements should be extensively used for both security and performance reasons.

c. Use minimum privileges

Make sure that application user has specific bare minimum rights on the database server. If the application user on the database uses ROOT/SA/dbadmin/dbo on the database then; it surely needs to be reconsidered if application user really needs such high amount of privileges or can they be reduced. Do not give the application user permission to access system stored procedures allow access to the ones that are user created.

d. Stored procedures

To secure an application against SQL injection, developers must never allow client-supplied data to modify the syntax of SQL statements. In fact, the best protection is to isolate the web application from SQL altogether. All SQL statements required by the application should be in stored procedures and kept on the database server. The application should execute the stored procedures using a safe interface such as Callable statements of JDBC or CommandObject of ADO.

CHAPTER 6

<u>DO A 'SKILL AUDIT' AT YOUR WORKPLACE - IT COULD BENEFIT YOU A LOT</u>

Whatever kind of role you are in whether permanent or contract, I have come to realise that it is good to what I call 'do an audit'. What I mean is for example is to take note of the various skills/strengths of the team or department you work in, and see where you can fill any skill gaps. Let me illustrate further.

Let's say you join a team of 20 programmers at Company X who all have varying skills and experience. Across the board you notice that most of the major programming languages are covered - C++, VB Script, Powershell and Java etc. However, you may notice that there seems to be a 'gap' when it comes to couple of the older technologies such as Pascal and Foxpro. These programs may not be 'popular', but still needed to maintain and support some legacy applications that Company X uses. My point is, that in a situation I just described you could help the skill gap by learning or sharpening up on your Pascal / Foxpro skills. By doing this, you would be increasing your value to your team and in turn company X. On one of my contracts, I was on a team of lads working on a large infrastructure project. After a little while I noticed that some guys were great at VMWare, Active Directory, Citrix and SQL. However for one reason or another they didn't have a strong Exchange person. Though Exchange wasn't my favourite product by any means, I took the opportunity to brush up on it. Over time I was able to assume more and more responsibility for this aspect of the project, and I ended up enjoying it quite alot. Whether you are a contractor or a permie, being aware and proactive in this manner can only be good for you. It is always good to try and specialise in what skills you enjoy using or are the best at. It isn't good just to do what the mainstream are doing, but it is always advantageous to have some niche skills up your sleeve. This will always help you in your career, because firms will always pay more for those skills that are hardest to find.

Throughout my career I have noticed how people have learned a particular technology/task become very valuable as a result. A good friend of mine comes to mind. When I was in the NHS, I was part of a small team supporting a hospital's network. There were about 4 of us..doing mainly 2nd/3rd line support on Windows 95/98 and NT4. Eventually we took on a young lad fresh out of college. He was eager to learn, but didn't have much IT experience. However as the months passed on, this guy just had a love of anything related networking and cabling. He really applied himself and started to learn about the different Cisco switches and routers - how to configure and install them. Within a year or two, this guy established himself as our network 'expert'. He became very valuable to our team because he had carved out a niche for himself. At times we were heavily dependent on him. He did very well. In fact we still keep in touch. He is now working as a technical author for a large networking company in Taiwan. I use these examples to encourage you to develop what I call 'depth of skill'. Learn to master a few things instead of having just average knowledge in many things. It is better to be an expert at something rather than a jack of all trades!

CHAPTER 7

WHAT IS SQL INJECTION

SQL Injection is one of the many web attack mechanisms used by hackers to steal data from organisations. It is perhaps one of the most common application layer attack techniques used today.

Web applications allow legitimate website visitors to submit and retrieve data to/from a database over the Internet using their preferred web browser.

Databases are central to modern websites - they store data needed for websites to deliver specific content to visitors and render information to customers, suppliers, employees and a host of stakeholders. User credentials, financial and payment information, company statistics may all be resident within a database and accessed by legitimate users through off-the-shelf and custom web applications. Web applications and databases allow you to regularly run your business.

SQL Injection is the hacking technique which attempts to pass SQL commands through a web application for execution by the backend database. If not santised properly, web applications may result in SQL Injection attacks that allow hackers to view information from the database and/or even wipe it out.

Such features as login pages, support and product request forms, feedback forms, search pages, shopping carts and the general delivery of dynamic content, shape modern websites and provide businesses with the means necessary to communicate with prospects and customers. These website features are all examples of web applications which may be either purchased off-the-shelf or developed as bespoke programs.

These website features are all susceptible to SQL Injection attacks.

SQL Injection: A Simple Example

Take a simple login page where a legitimate user would enter his username and password combination to enter a secure area to view his personal details or upload his comments in a forum.

When the legitimate user submits his details, an SQL query is generated from these details and submitted to the database for verification. If valid, the user is allowed access. In other words, the web application that controls the login page will communicate with the database through a series of planned commands so as to verify the username and password combination. On verification, the legitimate user is granted appropriate access.

Through SQL Injection, the hacker may input specifically crafted SQL commands with the intent of bypassing the login form barrier and seeing what lies behind it. This is only possible if the inputs are not properly sanitised (i.e., made invulnerable) and sent directly with the SQL query to the database. SQL Injection vulnerabilities provide the means for a hacker to communicate directly to the database.

The technologies vulnerable to this attack are dynamic script languages including ASP, ASP.NET, PHP, JSP, and CGI. All an attacker needs to perform an SQL Injection hacking attack is a web browser, knowledge of SQL queries and creative guess work to important table and field names. The sheer simplicity of SQL Injection has fuelled its popularity.

Why is it possible to pass SQL queries directly to a database that is hidden behind a firewall and any other security mechanism?

Firewalls and similar intrusion detection mechanisms provide little or no defense against full-scale SQL Injection web attacks.

Since your website needs to be public, security mechanisms will allow public web traffic to communicate with your web application/s (generally over port 80/443). The web application has open access to the database in order to return (update) the requested (changed) information.

In SQL Injection, the hacker uses SQL queries and creativity to get to the database of sensitive corporate data through the web application.

SQL or Structured Query Language is the computer language that allows you to store, manipulate, and retrieve data stored in a relational database (or a collection of tables which organise and structure data). SQL is, in fact, the only way that a web application (and users) can interact with the database. Examples of relational databases include Oracle, Microsoft Access, MS SQL Server, MySQL, and Filemaker Pro, all of which use SQL as their basic building blocks.

POWERSHELL SQL

SQL commands include SELECT, INSERT, DELETE and DROP TABLE. DROP TABLE is as ominous as it sounds and in fact will eliminate the table with a particular name.

In the legitimate scenario of the login page example above, the SQL commands planned for the web application may look like the following:

> ➢ SELECT count(*)
> ➢ FROM users_list_table
> ➢ WHERE username='FIELD_USERNAME'
> ➢ AND password='FIELD_PASSWORD"

In plain English, this SQL command (from the web application) instructs the database to match the username and password input by the legitimate user to the combination it has already stored.

POWERSHELL SQL

Each type of web application is hard coded with specific SQL queries that it will execute when performing its legitimate functions and communicating with the database. If any input field of the web application is not properly sanitised, a hacker may inject additional SQL commands that broaden the range of SQL commands the web application will execute, thus going beyond the original intended design and function.

A hacker will thus have a clear channel of communication (or, in layman terms, a tunnel) to the database irrespective of all the intrusion detection systems and network security equipment installed before the physical database server.

Is my database at risk to SQL Injection?

SQL Injection is one of the most common application layer attacks currently being used on the Internet. Despite the fact that it is relatively easy to protect against SQL Injection, there are a large number of web applications that remain vulnerable.

According to the Web Application Security Consortium (WASC) 9% of the total hacking incidents reported in the media until 27th July 2006 were due to SQL Injection. More recent data from our own research shows that about 50% of the websites we have scanned this year are susceptible to SQL Injection vulnerabilities.

It may be difficult to answer the question whether your web site and web applications are vulnerable to SQL Injection especially if you are not a programmer or you are not the person who has coded your web applications.

POWERSHELL SQL

Our experience leads us to believe that there is a significant chance that your data is already at risk from SQL Injection.

Whether an attacker is able to see the data stored on the database or not, really depends on how your website is coded to display the results of the queries sent. What is certain is that the attacker will be able to execute arbitrary SQL Commands on the vulnerable system, either to compromise it or else to obtain information.

If improperly coded, then you run the risk of having your customer and company data compromised.

What an attacker gains access to also depends on the level of security set by the database. The database could be set to restrict to certain commands only. A read access normally is enabled for use by web application back ends.

Even if an attacker is not able to modify the system, he would still be able to read valuable information.

What is the impact of SQL Injection?

Once an attacker realizes that a system is vulnerable to SQL Injection, he is able to inject SQL Query / Commands through an input form field. This is equivalent to handing the attacker your database and allowing him to execute any SQL command including DROP TABLE to the database!

An attacker may execute arbitrary SQL statements on the vulnerable system. This may compromise the integrity of your database and/or expose sensitive information. Depending on the back-end database in use, SQL injection vulnerabilities lead to varying levels of data/system access for the attacker. It may be possible to manipulate existing queries, to UNION (used to select related information from two tables) arbitrary data, use subselects, or append additional queries.

In some cases, it may be possible to read in or write out to files, or to execute shell commands on the underlying operating system.[break][break]Certain SQL Servers such as Microsoft SQL Server contain stored and extended procedures (database server functions). If an attacker can obtain access to these procedures it

Unfortunately the impact of SQL Injection is only uncoveredwhen the theft is discovered. Data is being unwittingly stolen through various hack attacks all the time. The more expert of hackers rarely get caught.

CHAPTER 8

SQL FROM NOTHING TO SOMETHING - A HANDS-ON BEGINNING TUTORIAL USING SQL SERVER EXPRESS EDITION

Why learn Structured Query Language (SQL)? One Simple reason: it's arguably the most widely used data manipulation language. Database Administrators and Application Developers use it daily for storing and retrieving data. Even non-technical staff may use it for reporting and analysis. Anyone with access to databases or reporting tools will find knowledge of SQL essential. Plus, working knowledge of SQL looks good on a resume.

In this tutorial, you won't merely read about SQL, you'll actually write and execute SQL queries on your own computer. Don't worry, it's easy. You will need an internet connection and enough hard drive space to install the needed software (not much). This tutorial will use Microsoft's SQL Server Express Edition. SQL Server is one of today's leading database programs. The free Express Edition provides enough functionality to get anyone started with SQL. It's probably the best place to start. To begin, type the following text into a search engine: "SQL Server Express 2008 Download" to download SQL Server Express Edition to your computer (follow the on-screen instructions).

After the file downloads, locate it on your computer and double-click it. This starts the installation. If prompted to run the file, do so. A variety of screens will open and close until the SQL Installation Center displays. Click "new installation" and follow the screens that appear. When prompted, enter an instance name of your choosing. One screen will ask for a user name and password. For the purposes of this tutorial, use your regular login information along with "Windows Authentication." Unfortunately, the installation process involves waiting. Get a snack or take a lap around the block. If an error occurs during installation, type the error message into a search engine to find a solution. When installation completes, you'll see a "complete" screen.

You're now very close to writing actual SQL. Find and open the program called "SQL Server Management Studio" in the Microsoft SQL Server folder of your start menu programs. Management Studio (often called "SSMS") provides an environment for writing SQL statements. When the program opens it will prompt you for a server name. Use the name you typed in for "instance name" during installation and make sure the "Authentication" box reads "Windows Authentication." Then click "connect."

Now you're in the main Management Studio screen. You should see the name of your instance in the "Object Explorer" box and probably a lot of blank space. At this point you're missing one vital piece, the most vital of all, and that's data. You need to load data to write SQL. Since most people don't have data lying around, you're probably wondering where to get some. Luckily, Microsoft has made a sample database, called "AdventureWorks" freely available at the following website: msftdbprodsamples.codeplex.com.

Find the appropriate sample database package (likely SQL Server 2008R2 or SQL Server 2008, look for the version that you installed) and click to download an installation file. Once you have downloaded an executable file, locate the file and double click it to install the sample database. Follow the onscreen instructions and choose the same instance name you typed in during installation. Your database should now contain plenty of data. Verify this by clicking on "Databases" in the "Object Explorer" of Management Studio. You should see a list of AdventureWorks databases. Now we're ready to write some SQL.

In the upper left corner, find a button called "new query" and click it. This opens a new window for writing SQL. Next, find a drop down box just below the "new query" button (it probably says "master") and select "AdventureWorks." This selects the database called "AdventureWorks" and any SQL you write will apply to this database.

Now click in the large blank space that opened up when you clicked "new query." We will finally write some SQL and see some data. Type the following SQL statement into the query window:

> SELECT *
> FROM Sales. Individual

POWERSHELL SQL

Now click the "Execute" button (just above the left side of the query window). Right below your query you should see columns of data appear. The SQL statement you entered asked the database to return everything (or "*", which roughly translates as "everything") from the Sales.Individual table. You have now officially typed SQL in your own database environment.

Let's look at one more SQL example. What if you don't want to see everything? Type the following into the query window:

SELECT CustomerID, ModifiedDate

FROM Sales.individual

This time when you click the "Execute" button only 2 rows of data appear. It should not surprise you that these columns correspond to the 2 rows in the SQL statement. In this case you're seeing a section of the data. SQL allows you to see what you choose.

You are now ready to take your SQL learning to the next level. Try to find some free online tutorials by typing "SQL Tutorial" into any search engine. Many good SQL books also exist. Search Amazon reviews for recommendations. This will help you know what to buy, or what not to buy.

CHAPTER 9

MICROSOFT SQL AZURE - MICROSOFT TAKES SQL DATABASES TO THE CLOUDS

A brand new Microsoft SQL technology just hit the marketplace on January 1, 2010. Or maybe it would be better to say that a re-branded Microsoft technology just hit the marketplace. Azure services is Microsoft's most significant step into cloud computing. It functions as a complete platform in the cloud with computing, storage and fabric-tying individual systems into an integrated network that can balance processing load or share resources.

What is SQL Azure?

The part that is most pertinent for this review is how Azure relates to SQL. Microsoft used to call this service SQL

Server Data Services and then SQL Services before recently changing it finally to SQL Azure. The name change just represents another step in the same direction that SQL server has already been headed with cloud computing.

SQL Azure provides data storage "in the cloud," much like Amazon S3 and many Google Apps. One of the big advantages for SQL Azure is that relational queries can be made against data stored in the cloud, regardless of whether they are structured, semi-structured or unstructured documents. Besides making data queries, users can also search, analyze, or synchronize with SQL data stored by Azure.

Once your information is uploaded to SQL Azure, applications can make direct queries to the data in the cloud through the Internet. This works for local or cloud-based applications (such as applications that run in the computing portion of Microsoft's Azure services). Provisionment and synchronization should be seamless between local SQL servers and the SQL Azure database. Microsoft also guarantees high fault tolerance by keeping multiple available copies of your data.

Why Use SQL Azure?

Microsoft claims that the major advantage SQL Azure provides is less maintenance. The service eliminates your need to store and manage SQL databases locally. In theory, administrators shouldn't have to install database software or worry about setup, patching and managing their server systems. Nor are there hardware needs with servers, disaster recovery, or high availability. Physical maintenance and administration is unnecessary, so companies can feasibly save on staffing costs as well. If the headache of managing database servers is getting to you, this may be a great option.

One of the other advantages is easy scalability. If you need to increase or decrease your database storage, Microsoft takes care of that too. This is one of the differences between SQL Azure and other hosting services: data storage is distributed between multiple nodes and you simply pay as you go for the storage used. SQL Azure can work as an adjunct to existing database hardware. If you expect a sudden spike in data needs or even want to be prepared in case one happens unexpectedly, Azure can be available for heavy times, but you can return to local or other storage when the need is gone.

Another advantage of scalability is that it provides workable but cost-effective service for the database needs of small and medium-sized businesses.

Microsoft also expects Azure services to enable independent software writers who want to offer their software as a service (SaaS). Azure services can provide for all of the computing needs this model requires, but of course, SQL Azure would meet the database needs for this software. Feasibly, this could even simplify data security, since Microsoft is responsible for storing it. Line of Business (LOB) applications built on Azure computing services could use SQL Azure in the same way.

As with any kind of cloud computing, one final advantage is that the information is available for any applications or queries as long as they are connected to the Internet. But one related benefit of moving SQL databases to the cloud is that it consolidates data (such as databases in multiple departments of a large company) and integrates information better. This should enable more complex queries that stretch across multiple database tables.

Putting all of these together, the simple advantage is an economy of scale: the cost of letting Microsoft do SQL should be easily less than the total cost of hardware, software, and maintenance (TCO).

It's All in the Details

Now the nitty-gritty. As far as programming model changes, most things stay the same, though a few details will be different. The core difference is that fully relational data has replaced an entity-based and ACE programming model. To access data, T-SQL is still the code, though developers will need to make a few changes to interact with the fully relational database service. Most data-access frameworks such as ADO.NET Data Services can still be used with minimal changes. Data transfer is through an XML-based format, the query language is T-SQL, and Tabular Data Stream is the protocol for internet access.

How is SQL Azure different from SQL Server? Azure works on top of SQL server. But SQL Azure also adds new relational data functions within the cloud. The biggest difference is as stated above -ease-of use, simplicity, and availability everywhere. The CTP is available for free on Microsoft's web-site, but get there fast. Some things will no longer be available for free at the end of January. Microsoft has made significant changes to the software in the last few months, and there are major differences in each of the production versions.

And what about pricing? Microsoft offers 1 GB of relational database space for $9.99/month, up to 10 GB for $99.99/month, and data transfer fees of 10 cents in and 15 cents per BG. There are also a few options: you can pay as you go with no monthly commitment and fee, or you can get better prices by committing to 6 months with a base fee.

No surprise-the new Azure services definitely represent Microsoft's commitment to the future of cloud computing. SQL

Azure is a huge part of this innovation and provides great support for web 2.0 applications. The greatest benefit is probably for small and medium-size businesses or independent software writers that need cost-effective storage and computing. If Microsoft's hunch about future computing is right (and it probably is), getting into the market first is a good strategy. It will only remain to be seen whether SQL Azure manages to stay the best cloud SQL database technology available.

CHAPTER 10

HOW TO RESTORE SQL DATABASE EASILY WITHOUT ANY DIFFICULTY?

MS SQL is an application produced by Microsoft which is used broadly for efficient data management by many organizations around the world and has really become an indispensable need of users all over. SQL or the Structured Query Language helps the users to query the databases and also to easily retrieve information from databases that had been made already. In this MS SQL Server, the files are saved in .mdf file format.

With SQL functioning normally, data management is matchlessly easy but the real trouble arises for the users when any problem comes in this SQL Server. If you are fed up of the SQL database corruption tension which is uncalled-for and also fed up of the unwanted impediment to your work because of it, then it is high time you get an SQL Server Restoring Database tool and immediately think - how to restore SQL database easily without any difficulty? Only a reliable SQL restoring database software can be the ideal tension releaser that will take away the data loss fear and give way to complete satisfaction.

Why SQL gets corrupted?

Causes of SQL Server corruption are actually the reasons requiring the need for SQL recovery. The corruption is sudden and can happen unexpectedly due to several reasons like:

- ➢ Problem in hard drive
- ➢ Improper and strange system shutdown accidentally
- ➢ Virus or Trojan attack

- ➢ Software or hardware malfunction
- ➢ Incorrect String to multi-client database along with user deletion of Log file or database in "suspected" mode
- ➢ No free disk space available while the working of SQL Server
- ➢ While MS SQL database is running, disk controllers trying to access or copy the file

These are other such abrupt and unanticipated reasons lead to SQL corruption. It is impossible to turn the time back and avoid such thing to happen. Only possibility with the user is to think How to Restore SQL if he using SQL 2005 and how to restore SQL 2000 if he is using SQL Server 2000.

Errors appearing at the time of corruption

A user can get one of the following errors at the time of SQL corruption:

POWERSHELL SQL

o Index '%ls' on '%ls' in database '%ls' may be corrupt because of expression evaluation changes in this release. Drop and re-create the index

o The file *.mdf is missing and needs to restore

o Server can't find the requested database table

o PageId in the page header = (0:0)

o Table Corrupt: Object ID 0, index ID 0, page ID (1:623)

o The process could not execute 'sp_replcmds' on server

o Internal error. Buffer provided to read column value is too small. Run DBCC CHECKDB to check for any corruption

o On changes table that was working .frm is locked

o The conflict occurred in database 'db_name', table 'table_name', column 'column_name'. The statement has been terminated o Corruption error of indexes, stored procedures, triggers and database integrity table that should be there .MYI file is not

Know how to restore SQL easily without any difficulty?

First and foremost thing which a user is required to do is to judge whether there is a need for an outside SQL restoring database tool or not. Professional help in the shape of an SQL Server recovery tool is required in case the user is getting any of the above errors because in that case recovery is only possible by using an outside software product. SysTools SQL recovery software is able to fix SQL server 2005 and 2000 database files easily without any difficulty.

Recovery happens easily because it requires no technical expertise and advanced system and software knowledge to perform successful SQL recovery. Just a few simple steps and you are through! Recovery happens without any difficulty because the process is smooth and there will be no complications arising during the SQL repair process. Also, the software is compatible with all the Windows Operating System versions like ME/NT/2000/XP/2003 and Vista.

SysTools is a technically superior group that does not require any mention as it is already recognized and well accepted data recovery company. It has generated and is continuing to produce numerous software tools for various types of data related troubles faced by users all over. One such software is the SQL Recovery software which helps Restore SQL Database contents.

CHAPTER 11

THE INS AND OUTS OF SQL INJECTION

In this chapter we'll look at how attackers use SQL injection for the purpose of damage or unauthorized access and how to protect you and your site against it.

What is SQL injection?

SQL injection is an extremely overlooked problem, especially with how easy it is for Joe Bloggs and John Smith to setup their own website and do with it what they wish. SQL injection is the equivalent of letting any old user manipulate your database, be it for malicious purposes or not. This dangerous flaw is easy to prevent, however it is easier to overlook. Every time your website or application commits an SQL query with input that is given to it from the user, it is a possibility for SQL injection if you are not safeguarded properly. Today we're going to learn how the SQL injection is done and how to prevent it in easy to swallow chunks, here we go...

Right, so how do you do it?

It's much simpler than it sounds, SQL injection is simply changing the query from what it was intended to do with it what you wish, let's skip the boring footwork and jump in head first. In order to 'do' SQL injection you need a vulnerable website or application, of course to demonstrate prevention and so on we need to use a language, surprise surprise the language we'll be using today is PHP coupled with it's wonderful brethren, MySQL. Consider this, you have a page called profile.php that when accessed properly will pull information about a certain user from your wonderfully crafted database. Let's say the query looks like this;

POWERSHELL SQL

- ➤ mysql_query("SELECT first_name,
- ➤ last_name
- ➤ FROM users
- ➤ WHERE user_id = '$_GET['id']'");

Seemingly harmless, when executed properly this query will pull two fields from a table called users. In order to wreak havoc inject SQL into this query we need to perform our own query, let's say for example; DROP TABLE users, seems only right. Obviously if we visited profile.php?id=123 then the query would look a little like this;

- ➤ mysql_query("SELECT first_name,
- ➤ last_name
- ➤ FROM users

WHERE user_id = '123'");

POWERSHELL SQL

Simple enough, this query will fetch the first name and last name of a user who has an ID of 123. Obviously not the best designed query as it'd be better to limit the amount of results etc but that is beyond the scope of this tutorial. Now let's say we change profile.php?id=123 to profile.php?id=DROP TABLE users. The query that is executed now looks something like this;

> mysql_query("SELECT first_name,
> last_name
> FROM users

WHERE user_id = 'DROP TABLE users'");

Pretty useless. All this query is doing is what's intended of it and searching for a record where the user_id is set to DROP TABLE users. To actually make our command execute, we need to 'escape' the friendly SQL query and insert our own query, I'd like to introduce the single quote ('). When you search for a string using SQL, in order to prevent the string from interfering with the query, it is wrapped in a set of single quotes. If we use a single quote in our query it suddenly becomes a little more interesting. Let's try 'DROP TABLE users.

```
mysql_query("SELECT first_name,

last_name

FROM users

WHERE user_id = "DROP TABLE users'");
```

What we have done is made it so that the string to search for is simply blank, by using a single quote we have closed the string and we are now inside the actual query, exciting isn't it? If you were to execute the above query all you'd receive back would be an error (although this varies depending on the PHP configuration). 'Great' I hear you saying, but one of the golden rules when trying to exploit something is learning to love error messages. One of the quickest ways to find out whether a site can be exploited is to slap a single quote in a few of the $_GET variables and see if you receive an error message. If you do then it's likely there's a gaping hole for you to ~~destroy~~ report to the local administrator. Of course this isn't always true, depending on many factors and should only be used as a quick first resort to check for vulnerability.

So we have an error message, awesome, we can manipulate the SQL query! Now the reason the above query didn't work is because it is read as a single command to execute, we're executing a SELECT command to select records from a database, shoving a DROP TABLE command in half way through isn't going to be expected and therefore it's going to cause a problem. The way we get round this is to close the SELECT command in order to inject our own SQL. The way to properly end a command in SQL is the same as with most languages, with a semi-colon, so all we need to do is end the previous command and then begin our own. One thing we need to remember is that the query we're ending mustn't cause an error because if it does then the error will stop the query and our command won't be reached. Let's inject.

```
mysql_query("SELECT first_name,

last_name

FROM users

WHERE user_id = ''; DROP TABLE users'");
```

We inserted '; DROP TABLE users. What we did was inserted an apostrophe to close the string followed by a semi-colon to end the query that's searching for the user, as far as anyone is concerned the first command in this query is valid, the second one however is not. Why? Because after our command there is a single apostrophe lingering from the first command where we injected. Uh oh. Our command won't be executed because there's an error in it now. Another hurdle that can be jumped, essentially we need to ignore everything after what we've injected, we don't care about it. In order to ignore the rest we have to use an SQL comment signified by two hyphens (-). Once two hyphens are read, the rest of the query is simply ignored and what we have is a successful command, before we comment out the rest of the query however, we need to end our command with the semi-colon. All in all our query now looks like this.

mysql_query("SELECT first_name,

last_name

FROM users

WHERE user_id = ''; DROP TABLE users;--'");

Voila, you've just upset a database administrator somewhere, congratulations. Now one thing we should touch on is getting around basic PHP/MySQL authorization with SQL injection.

Correct login OR 1=1?

Some (very) weak PHP login scripts that use a MySQL database use the actual query to check authorization rather than querying the database and then doing some playing with the results. Here's an example of an extremely weak query;

myqsl_query("SELECT user_id

FROM users

WHERE username = '".$username."' AND password = '".$password."'");

Now the reason people might use this query for authorization is that when the username and password specified are found in the database the above query will return TRUE, well actually it'll return the user_id but for our example we'll just assume that the PHP code just checks for any returned value. If the user isn't found, the query will evaluate theoretically to FALSE. With this information in mind we already know that in order to get round this authorization, what we need is the query to return true - we can do this with some more SQL injection.

Assuming that the above query is used in the PHP code, we need to inject something that will make the query return true (or a value) no matter what credentials we supply. Well first we need to break into this query, there are two possibilities here; username and password, we're going to use username. Now we know where we're going to break into the query we need to make it return true, what will always return true?... 1=1. We need to tell MySQL to evaluate 1=1 rather than the username and password, to do that we're going to use a little boolean algebra and use OR. Let's see what this looks like with the username field injected;

POWERSHELL SQL

myqsl_query("SELECT user_id

FROM users

WHERE username = '' OR 1=1;--' AND password = '".$password."'");

By inserting a single quote, we escape from the username comparison and we're now in the SQL query as we've previously learned. The next thing we do is insert an OR clause, this checks to see if the username is blank OR 1=1 and of course we then need to end this command and comment out the rest. Voila.

Now it's all well and good being able to conduct SQL injection, but now it's time to move on to the more important matter...

Countering SQL injection

It's important to understand how the attackers will attempt to use SQL injection to attack your website in order to understand where the threats/weaknesses lie so we can use this knowledge to secure these flaws. You might be expecting paragraph upon paragraph of information on countering this threat but in reality you can protect yourself against it easily.

As with all input that PHP uses, it should be sanitized to ensure it can not interfere where it shouldn't. The obvious method for protection is to simply remove all single quotes from a string or simply display an error if they are used, but this can cause problems when you apply it to a website that needs to display single quotes such as a review website or forum where you need to use words like can't and don't etc.

Note: It's important to remember that the great thing about PHP is people can solve things in their own way, everyone has their own preferred method for countering SQL injection and this just happens to be the way I've chosen to convey to you.

Escaping characters

In order to use certain characters safely in a query, we need to escape them. This means prepending then evil character with a backslash, so ' becomes \' and for extra safety, \ becomes \\. Now finding all the evil characters and putting backslashes in front of them might seem a bit of a chore, but PHP has a few handy functions that can help us. One of the most common is the addslashes() and stripslashes() functions. It is as simple as it sounds, addslashes() will add slashes before your evil characters and stripslashes() will take them away. Simple as that. Here's a quick example;

```
$evil_name = "dan' OR 1=1;--";

$password = "abc123"

mysql_query("SELECT *
```

```
FROM users

WHERE
username="'".addslashes($evil_name)."'"
AND
password="'".addslashes($password)."'");
```

This query should now be safe to run as the quotes in the original name have been escaped, the username now looks like this: dan\' OR 1=1'- which is not harmful to our query. Although there are many methods in which to prevent SQL injection, we're just going to look at one more function provided by PHP and that's mysql_real_escape_string(). This function has a little sister called mysql_escape_string(), the difference is that mysql_real_escape_string() takes into account the current character set used in the connection to the database. Using the same method as above, the query would look like this;

```
$evil_name = "dan' OR 1=1;--";
```

POWERSHELL SQL

$password = "abc123"

mysql_query("SELECT *

FROM users

WHERE
username='".mysql_real_escape_string($evil
_name)."' AND mysql_real_escape_string
='".addslashes($password)."'");

CHAPTER 12

IBM ISERIES AS/400 SQL PERFORMANCE

1. Introduction

Recently I made a few tests at a client's site on SQL performance with large volumes of data. I found quite interesting results that I summarise below.

2. Application Description

The client is a financial company which stores large volumes of data for a Basel application which provides a month by month situation of the contracts. The data are used for some standard reporting and also for non standard OLAP inquiries requested especially by Credit control users

The application updates 7 different physical files which are joined together in a join LF called BASUNICO1L which has a total record length of 1789 characters. The main keys of this file are the processing period (YYYYMM) and the contract number

3. Test Environment

The tests were made in a test environment where the files contained the data of about 6 months. The total number of records for the join LF were approximately 11 million and those of the period used for the test were about 2 millions.

The first set of tests were made to test the times needed to copy all records of one period from the join logical file to a physical file with the same record layout. The record were written by using three different approaches as follows:

A simple copyfile (CPYF) which includes a selection such as INCREL(*IF PERIOD *EQ 200806)

A traditional (file oriented) Cobol program (TSTFIL1) which used a START to position the file pointer to the first record of the period and then entered into a loop of READ and WRITE operations to write to the output file all records of the requested period.

A Cobol program with embedded SQL (TSTSQL1) which wrote the output records with a simple SQL Insert of the selected records.

A Cobol program with embedded SQL (TSTSQL3) which created the output file as an SQL MQT table. A second set of test was used instead to test the times needed to read some fields of the files by using different approaches as follows:

Traditional file oriented Cobol program (TSTFIL5) which performed a START to position the cursor and then used sequential READ operations of all records of the selected period. Cobol program with embedded SQL (TSTSQL5) which included an SQL cursor to read all lines of the selected period. I decided to perform the tests in the following different conditions:

- In an environment without additional indexes (i.e only the access paths of the files)

- In an environment that could use also additional SQL indexes

- In an environment that used an SQL logical view instead of the original join logical file

- The results are described in the following points

4. Tests based only on the join logical file

The test made in the original environment to copy about 2 million records without SQL indexes were the following:

- The CPYF took 19 minutes and 35 seconds

- The traditional file oriented Cobol program took 9 minutes and 20 seconds

- The Cobol program with embedded SQL took 28 minutes

5. Tests done after the creation of SQL indexes

I checked the index advisor file QSYS2/SYSIXADV after the initial tests and I noticed that there was a record suggesting to create an index on the period field. I created both a vector index and a radix index and then started the new set of tests. The results were the following:

- The CPYF took 7 minutes and 52 seconds

- The traditional file oriented Cobol program took 7 minutes and 7 seconds

-The Cobol program with embedded SQL took 13 minutes and 20 secons

- There has been a clear benefit especially for the Cobol program with embedded SQL. By loooking at the log, I noticed that the optimiser had chosen to use the vector index during that execution.

It is interesting that if you use the commands WRKOBJ or DSPFD or DSPDBR, the indexes appear as logical files with a special SQL type attribute which has the value INDEX.

It is also interesting that the space used for the indexes is much less than what is required for a logical file. In my test environment one of the main the PF used about 500 Mega bytes, a LF used about 257 Mega bytes, the radix index used occupied about 175 Mega bytes and the radix index only 22 Mega bytes.

6. Test of the file creation with as an MQT (Materialised query table)

I tried to create the target file by using a Cobol program with embedded SQL that produced the output table as an MQT instead of the previous INSERT and I found that the time were very good

The program took just 57 seconds to produce the results.

7. Reading Test

I compared the time spent by two programs to read from all records of a selected period to sum up a total The first program was a Cobol traditional file oriented program, whereas the second one was an SQL Cobol which included an SQL cursor to read all selected records.

The first program took 13 minutes and 17 seconds to complete, whereas the second one took on the first execution just 7 minutes and 14 seconds to complete and much less in following ones.

8, Using SQL Views instead of Logical files

I tried to use an SQL view equivalent to the logical file and repeat the tests above by using the SQL view. The results were not significantly different than those based on the logical file, however I found that a view required much less space than an equivalent LF.

The SQL views appear again to the system as special logical files with the SQL type attribute containing the value VIEW. The space occupied by the view logical files is much less than that required by a logical file. In my test environment a view equivalent to a join logical file of about 405 Mega bytes. required less than 1 Mega byte.

9. Conclusions

The tests described above seem to demonstrate what follows:

The fastest option to extract the data was the Cobol program with an embedded SQL to create a MQT table.

POWERSHELL SQL

The traditional file oriented Cobol program was faster than the corresponding Cobol program which included an embedded SQL INSERT statement. The execution time of the Cobol SQL program was significantly affected by the creation of the SQL vector index.

The traditional file oriented Cobol program that read all records of a selected period by using START and READ NEXT operations was slower than the Cobol program which read the records with an SQL cursor.

The results agree with some points of an IBM Redbook Modernizing IBM eServer iSeries Application Data Access - A Roadmap Cornerstone (redbooks.ibm.com/abstracts/sg246393.html? Open). where it is written that:

The SQL insert operations are slower than Cobol write statement because SQL operations include more validations than write oprrations into a DDS PF SQL does faster reads than HLL operations. The main reason is that a cursor reading an SQL table does not have the extra data cleansing code like a DDS PF reading. Using SQL views instead of logical files should allow a significant reduction of the space occupation. The final conclusion is that a wise use of SQL can bring significant improvements in applications performance.

CHAPTER 13

MICROSOFT ACCESS TO SQL SERVER MIGRATION

The ease of use and power of Microsoft Access comes at a price. As a company or the functionality required grows, the issues of data security, reliability, and system management become increasingly problematic. The volumes and functionality requirements of an Access database will often exceed the original concept.

Database migration is then essential for administration systems so that they can be provided with a more secure and robust environment.

By keeping the application within the Microsoft family of products (Microsoft Access and MSSQL), and engaging an experienced consultant, the upgrade process can be manageable and cost effective.

MSSQL Maintenance

Before your upsizing project is deployed, there should be an administrative plan in place for the new MSSQL system. The database administrator (DBA) needs to create backup strategies, recovery, administrative procedures, automation, optimisation, etc. For the small company, there is the option of using a high speed network connection to the SQL Server database of an Internet Service Provider. This may prove a cost effective alternative to avoid the maintenance overhead.

Linking Microsoft Access to MSSQL

One of the upsizing options for MSAccess is to continue using the forms, reports, macros and code you have already have - and replace the MSAccess BackEnd database with a SQL Server database. This allows the best of both worlds: the ease of use of an existing MSAccess database FrontEnd - with the reliability, speed and security of MSSQL.

MSAccess has the ability to Link (using ODBC) to an SQL Server database for the table data. All table data is moved to the SQL Server database, leaving all forms, reports, queries and logic in the existing Access database. Because the existing application logic is largely unchanged, this is the most cost-effective migration technique. For a small effort, the benefits (reliability, security, maintenance, etc) of SQL Server can be achieved.

The disadvantage of this approach is that all access to the SQL Server database occurs through the Microsoft Jet engine. The Jet engine must translate every query and data access operation to MSSQL compliant commands. This adds overhead in performance, and additional MSSQL license connections are required.

This alternative is the best and cheapest for Microsoft Access applications with a small number of users.

Using ActiveX Data Objects (ADO)

For greater efficiency, some of the SQL Server Tables may need to be accessed using the ADO and OLEDB (replaces ODBC) technologies. Some changes are needed - the Jet database engine uses different data types, and a different SQL grammar from SQL Server.

A combination of Linking small Tables and using ADO for large Tables is most practicable. This can be a phased implementation, as one by one the inefficiencies in Linked Table usage are identified.

Access Data Projects (ADP)

ADP is an alternative to the usual File/Server configuration with an Access Front-End and an Access Back-End database. The user-friendly Forms and Reports, as well as the VBA are managed as before in an Access ADP Front-End database. Using a Client/Server configuration, all Tables and Queries are stored in an SQL Server database. The advantage of this arrangement is the ability to use the highly efficient Views and Stored Procedures of SQL Server. Most of the work is handled on the Server, minimising Network traffic and the consequent bottlenecks.

The ADP Front-End uses SQL Server 2008 Express (SSX) as the Back-End database. The SSX database is free, and can be readily migrated to the full-blown version of MSSQL. Using ADP initially will avoid any problems of a later migration.

ADP may be superseded by SharePoint, so this may not be the best option. Also, there have been few ADP enhancements over the last 10 years. It would seem that support has been dropped and this option is a dead-end.

Using.NET technologies

If Microsoft Access is no longer able to keep up with an organisation's requirements, the project will have to be redesigned from scratch. New technologies such as Visual Basic.Net and ASP.Net can be used to rewrite the application.

The key advantage of this approach is flexibility. You can create an application that can target Windows desktops or the Web. It is perfectly feasible and cost effect to use an ASP.Net Website for an administration system, especially where the users are geographically dispersed.

SQL Server Express 2008 Express (SSE or SSX)

MS SQL 2008 Express is a scaled down, free edition of SQL Server. MS SQL Express makes it easy to develop applications that need database management capabilities.

MS SQL 2008 Express comes in 3 editions:

- ➢ MS SQL 2008 Express - just the basic database engine
- ➢ MS SQL 2008 Express with Tools - includes Management Studio
- ➢ MS SQL 2008 Express with Advanced Services

The Advanced Services edition is full-featured and includes Full Text Search, Reporting Services and Report Designer. It also has an Import and Export Wizard, making it easy to transfer data from a Microsoft Access database to an SQL Server 2008 Express database.

There are no limitations on the number of databases or users. SQL Server 2008 Express is however limited to one processor, 1 GB memory (the excess will not be used) and 10 GB database files. This should be sufficient for the upgrade of small Microsoft Access systems. Note that SQL Server 2008 Express can only work with other 2008 versions.

SQL Server Express is ideal for the small company and also for the Microsoft Visual Basic developer. If data volumes or the traffic increases, the live system can be readily migrated to the full blown version of SQL Server.

Neville Silverman, based in Sydney Australia, has been a Visual Basic programmer and Microsoft Access programmer and Database design specialist for many years.

POWERSHELL SQL

He has created numerous Microsoft Access databases, SQL Server Databases and Microsoft Visual Basic systems for clients. He develops and supports software systems for the small to medium sized business. Administrative systems are custom built to fit company requirements - software solutions that are cost effective, efficient and user-friendly.

Optimising Access Database systems is his speciality. He has extended the useful life of many an Access Database system, avoiding the effort and cost of an SQL Server upgrade.

CHAPTER 14

<u>STUDYING FOR 1Z0-047: ORACLE DATABASE SQL EXPERT</u>

1Z0-047 is one of the more popular Oracle certifications available. SQL knowledge is extremely useful in the IT industry and being acknowledged as an expert in this skill is a valuable addition to a resume. That said, this is not an easy exam to pass and I have seen several people in certification forums admit to failing it on one or more attempts. This chapter is intended to give you a glimpse into some of what will be expected from you on the test to help guide your preparation.

All of the topics that will be covered in the 1Z0-047 exam are listed on the Oracle Education website. There are capabilities in Oracle SQL that are not on that list, but they will not show up on the test. The topic lists

from Oracle Education are always complete.
The SQL Expert exam has thirty-eight topics
that are also in the 1Z0-051 SQL
Fundamentals exam. The expert test does
not focus on these. Anything from them is
fair game, but the majority of the questions
will come from the thirty-eight subject areas
that are specific to 1Z0-047. If you are
trying for this certification, your knowledge
of basic SQL should be a given.

As you would expect, almost every question
in 1Z0-047 will have a SQL statement
involved. Sometimes the question will
contain a statement and you will have to
choose among answers that indicate what it
does. Other questions will describe a desired
result and the available answers will consist
of different SQL statements. You will have
to choose the SQL that best fits the request.
The SQL tends to be longer than what is in
the SQL Fundamentals exam and relatively
heavy on joins. For the test you need to be
proficient at ANSI join syntax -- the legacy
Oracle syntax will not be used. You also
need to have the ability to parse SQL in your

head and determine what it will do. Most of the SQL in this test will execute without error but will not produce the intended results. This is much harder to detect than SQL that will simply fail when run.

You must be very knowledgeable about SQL syntax and be able to differentiate between what is possible and what is not. Some of the questions are likely to have SQL that is perfectly legal, but which is written in a way that might lead you to believe it is not. There are a number of legitimate ways to create SQL statements that hardly anyone ever uses. An example would be a HAVING clause placed before a GROUP BY clause. This will work, but I have never seen anyone write SQL that way. You'll also need to recognize common SQL functions and be able to determine what the outcome of DDL statements will be. You'll need to be familiar with several topics on subjects that even experienced SQL developers use rarely if at all. I've written SQL for seventeen years and have never used a ROLLUP or CUBE query yet in the workplace. I use REGEXP functions and hierarchical queries once in a blue moon. You'll need to know all of these to do well on the test.

As to the SQL Expert exam itself, there will be 70 multiple-choice or multiple-answer questions. At this time 66 percent is the passing score. For the multiple-answer questions, there is no partial credit. Not answering a question counts against your score as much as answering one incorrectly, so you don't want to leave any question unanswered -- even if that means simply picking a letter at random. 1Z0-047 contains a much higher number of exhibits than the norm for Oracle certification exams. They are primarily entity relationship diagrams that provide background on the tables referenced by the SQL in the questions. You must be able to read entity relationship diagrams even though this is not listed as a test topic. Many of the diagrams are fairly complex and only a tiny portion of the diagram is really crucial to answering any given question. In addition, when I took the test, using the exhibit was not required for more than half of the questions that had them. The questions that have exhibits suggest that you view the diagram and then answer the question, but I would suggest reading the question first. This is likely to save you some time as you may be able to skip the exhibit entirely. If you do need to view it, you will know specifically what information you need to look for. When dealing with questions where the answer is one or more SQL statements, look though all of the answers. Often you can find at least one with a flaw that rules it out as a correct answer. Ruling out one or two of the answers will allow you to concentrate your efforts on the remaining possibilities.

1Z0-047 is intended to pass only those people who really have a thorough understanding of SQL, and it does a good job of that. You'll find on this test that the wrong answers are not obviously wrong and the right answer does not stand out. The SQL and associated exhibits are reasonably complex and a fair number of the questions test your experience rather than your ability to memorize facts. Make sure you are comfortable with all seventy-six topics before scheduling the exam.

SQL SERVER TUTORIALS

The MS SQL server tutorials provide all the details needed for understanding the databases and how they perform. The user must know what SQL server is and what is required to make full use of it. SQL server 2008 and SQL server 2000 are the most widely used applications.

SQL Server: The tutorials about SQL Server have lessons about the server, different editions, how to create database, creating table, adding data, designer, views, stored procedures, logins, linked servers, and integration services. Basically the MS SQL server is a management system that is created to work on different platforms like laptops or large servers. It is used as the backend system for many websites and it can help a number of users. There are many tools that help in maintenance of database and other tasks like programming.

Server: The database systems that are based on server are programmed in such a way that they run with the help of a central server and any number of users will be able to have access to the data at the same time with the help of an application. The users can do multiple tasks like accessing the data, updating of data, and anything that they want to do. SQL server has features that help the application in all its functions.

Editions: There are many editions to SQL server 2008 and the user will choose the one that suits his requirements. For a free database management, the user will choose the Express or Compact edition. There is also an Evaluation edition which permits the user to try the Server 2008 for about 180 days. Some of the notable editions of SQL Server 2008 are:

Enterprise edition that has better availability and security for applications related to business; Standard edition that provides easy management of data management and to run departmental applications; workgroup edition for secured synchronization at the remote end, and to run branch applications; Developer edition that can be made use of by one user in testing, developing, and demonstrating the programs in any number of systems; Web edition for web hosters; Express edition for learning purposes; Compact edition meant for applications for desk tops, mobile services and web customers; and Evaluation edition for evaluating the purposes till the trial period is over.

Creating database: SQL server makes use of SQL Server Management Studio as the console for administration. It helps in creating databases, views, tables and so on, and to access the data, configuring the accounts, and to transfer data to other databases. The Object Explorer guides the user to databases and to files. The user can get results by writing queries on data. Any amount of databases can be created with SQL server Management. After creating a database, the user can change the configuration of the database with the help of options available. Tables can also be created with the help of the options. The user can control the type of data in each column and thus have integrity of the data maintained. Options such as editing and adding data are also available to the user. Re-entering the data is facilitated by writing a SQL script. The user can use and run the SQL query for inserting data, updating it or deleting it.

Query designer: This interface permits the user to create queries to be run against the database and to create queries which will include views or tables. It is very useful for the beginners who want to learn to use SQL as the syntax need not be remembered for creating queries.

View: A view in SQL server is store din the database and when run, it permits the user to see the outcome of it from multiple databases. This is particularly useful when many users want to access the data at various levels. They can have access to specific rows or columns of a table.

Stored procedures: These are of great value to the programmers when they work on databases. The programmers can make the procedures work from either the SQL Server management or any other application based on their requirement. The advantages of the stored procedures are many, such as quicker execution, less traffic, and security. The user can configure SQL server security accounts, create linked servers, database maintenance, create scheduled jobs, replication, text search and many more.

Logins: SQL Server helps in creating user logins for every individual who wants to access the server. Based on the requirement of the user, the logins can be created to enable access. Not everyone should be provided with access to server role. The server role is useful for performing any task in the server, create options of configuration, help in managing logins and permissions, and managing files.

Database Schema: It is a means of grouping the data and works as a container. The user can be assigned permission to a single schema so that he can access only the ones that they are permitted to. The schemes can be configured in a database. Linked Servers permit the users to connect to another server remotely.

MS SQL server is a very effective application useful in manipulating the data. Any website that has more data will make use of the server for effective functioning.

CHAPTER 15

FILESTREAM CORRUPTION IN SQL - A PHENOMENAL SQL DATABASE RECOVERY SOLUTION!

The process of storing and managing unstructured data was poor, prior to SQL Server 2008 release.

Earlier Approaches of Storing Unstructured Data

Before the release of SQL 2008, there were two approaches of storing unstructured data. One approach was of storing data in a VARBINARY or IMAGE column. This had transactional consistency and also reduced data managing complexities, but it was performance wise. The other approach was to store unstructured data as disk files and to store the file location in the table along with some structured data linked to it. This approach was good in terms of performance, but did not ensure transactional consistency.

FILESTREAM Feature - Efficient Storage of Unstructured Data

FILESTREAM feature was introduced with SQL Server 2008 for storing and managing unstructured data efficiently. This feature allows storing of BLOB data (like word documents, music file, image files, videos etc) in the NTFS file system. It ensures transactional consistency between the unstructured data (stored in NTFS) and the structured data (stored in table).

FILESTREAM Corruption - Error 7904

Sometimes, when you try to restore MS SQL 2008 database (MDF files) from transaction log backups, database gets damaged. You fail to perform restoration and thus MDF files become inaccessible resulting in data loss. Under such problem, you might encounter the error:

POWERSHELL SQL

"FILESTREAM corruption - missing files, error 7904." At that time, if you want to regain access of your mission critical MDF files, you must perform SQL database recovery process using an appropriate MDF File Recovery solution.

Original Database Might Not Be Corrupted

The database corrupted when you tried to restore the database from transaction log backups but the original database, from which the backup of transaction was taken, do not damages in most of the cases. In most of these cases, corruption happens on the database that was restored from a sequence of backup logs. The original database might not corrupt. "7904 16 2 Table error: The FILESTRWEAM file for "FileID" was not found." You can get back your valuable data using a fine SQL Database Recovery Solution to recover corrupt SQL database contents from corrupt MDF files.

POWERSHELL SQL

A Phenomenal SQL Database Recovery Solution

SysTools SQL Recovery tool is perhaps the easiest and most efficient SQL database recovery tools available around. This MDF file recovery software performs an extensive scan of damaged databases to recover all database items like tables, reports, forms, triggers, stored procedures, etc. If you choose to repair SQL DB and recover corrupt SQL database using SysTools SQL Recovery tool then you will be gifted with a very simple interface which won't require you to have any prior technical skills to execute the SQL recovery process. The software also has a read-only nature which helps to regain original contents of SQL database. In short, SysTools SQL Recovery software is a phenomenal SQL Database Recovery Solution.

CHAPTER 16

THE KEY FEATURES OF MICROSOFT SQL SERVER 2005

Microsoft SQL training is important to learn all about the different versions of this program. And, once the class is taken it is important for technicians to continue their education when new versions of SQL are available. For example, SQL 2005 training is necessary for techs to understand all the ins and outs of the Microsoft SQL Server 2005. It is worthwhile to take SQL 2005 training classes because it keeps you up to date and improves your income. When you take a class of this nature you will learn about some of the key features of Microsoft SQL 2005.

T SQL, also known as Transact-SQL is a variant of SQL and is used in the Microsoft SQL Server. This additional syntax helps in stored procedures. TDS, Tabular Data

Stream, is what both Microsoft SQL Server and Sybase/ASE use to communicate. This was also incorporated into the FreeTDS project so that more Microsoft SQL Server and Sybase databases could communicate. The most recent version is SQL Server 2005. This supports the connectivity to Web services SOAP protocol. What this means is those clients that do not use windows can communicate across the SQL Server. There is also a certified JDBC driver that was released by Microsoft that allows Java applications to communicate to the Microsoft SQL Server 2000 and 2005.

This server includes clustering and mirroring of databases. Basically, an SQL server cluster is several servers that are configured identically. This allows multiple servers to take their part of the workload. There is an identical virtual server name given to all of the servers so that it is made into the IP address. Data partioning is also support for distributed databases for the SQL server. The SQL Server 2005 also introduced database mirroring. This means that replicas of the information in the database could be saved on another SQL Server. The creation of snapshots is also allowed on the SQL Server 2005. This basically a backup image that is saved in case it is needed.

Merge replication was also available that allows for synchronization of the database when other servers participated in the replication. The changes in databases happen independently but in merge replication they are synchronized on all the databases. There is also support built in for conflict resolution. The support network introduced for SQL Server 2005 is .NET Framework. This allows for any of the stored procedures to be written into .Net language.

CHAPTER 17

UNDERSTANDING SQL WEB HOSTING

Before understanding the concept of SQL web hosting, it's necessary to have a basic grasp on what SQL is, and also how web hosting works.

SQL is the acronym for Structured Query Language, which is a computer language that is used to manipulate data in a database. SQL works with many different database systems, such as Access, Oracle and MS SQL. SQL is widely used due to it's simplicity and applicability to diverse database functions, many of which make up global business systems and commercial computer software.

Web Hosting is a service provided by a company that leases server space to companies or individuals that have web pages they want to display on the internet. Web hosts provide the necessary bandwidth and technology to allow internet users to access these web pages. While anyone can create a web page, special servers dedicated to internet connectivity and hosting are required to make the web page active.

Therefore, SQL web hosting is a service that allows SQL databases to be hosted on the internet. SQL web hosting can be used to store database information on the web, allow offsite personal to access database management tools and provide detailed information to customers or clients. Typical applications that use SQL databases are ERP (Enterprise Resource Planning) and CRM (Customer Relationship Management) programs.

What are the Benefits of SQL Web Hosting

There are several advantages to investing in an SQL web hosting service rather than relying on a standard web host. If you require a web based database, you will quickly come to appreciate these benefits:

Increased RAM and Bandwidth - Typically, database applications take up a lot of memory and server space. SQL web hosting services provide additional room for your database to evolve and grow over time.

SQL Administration Services - Because SQL web hosting services are dedicated to database hosting, they generally have the ability to offer advanced administration services to keep your database running smoothly and at optimum performance.

Technical Assistance and SQL Design - If you're new to SQL, many SQL web hosting services provide technical assistance and design packages for an additional cost when you purchase web hosting.

Things to Look for in a Quality SQL Web Hosting Service

Once you've decided to go with an SQL web host, you'll need to select a service. There are a lot of providers currently on the market, and sometimes it's difficult to tell them apart. A quality SQL web hosting service should offer you the following:

- ➤ Reliability
- ➤ Control Panel Options
- ➤ Technical Support
- ➤ Customer Support
- ➤ Multiple Hosting Plans

Overall, if you plan on maintaining a database online, your best option is to go with a web hosting service that has servers dedicated specifically to SQL applications. Doing so will ensure that you get the most value out of your investment. SQL web hosting may cost a little more than standard hosting, but it's worth every penny.

CHAPTER 18

PERFECTLY NEW DATABASE QUERY TOOL - FOXY SQL PRO RELEASED

Are you a database professional? Do you work with a lot of databases? Do you use an SQL code? Do you want to connect to a new database to physically create its structure in no time and with ease? Are you tired of having to handle several client applications?

If your answer is "yes" to any of these questions, I recommend you to go on reading this chapter.

Let's imagine you work with let's say three databases. Whenever you feel the need to connect to the database and execute SQL code, you will probably have to use another third party software (also client software) that allows you to do it.

POWERSHELL SQL

There are a lot of different client softwares in the market. However, they allow users either to connect to one certain database, e.g. MS SQL, or provide only one available connection, e.g. ODBC. However, what if you work with not only one database... So, there would be no wonder if you had to use three client applications for each of the databases to be able to communicate with them and simply do your job. In practice it also means that you have to get used to three different interfaces and learn how to deal with different features, which is, let's face it, pretty far from being an ideal state (not speaking of expenses, time and your efficiency provided you are switching among three different environments. Thank goodness you work only with three databases and not five, seven or more!)

Nevertheless, today might be the last day for such headaches. CHARONWARE, s.r.o., a software company specializing in developing database modeling tools, has announced release of its perfectly new product Foxy SQL Pro version 1.0 – Database Script and Query Tool.

"Foxy SQL Pro is a useful database query tool allowing database professionals to execute SQL commands and queries against any database, see and store the results and much more. It is mainly focused on a possibility to parse complete SQL script into each individual commands that can be then executed according to the user's selection," introduces the product Vaclav Frolik, Charonware's Sales and Marketing Manager.

Reading Charonware's website, it seems like Foxy SQL Pro can replace many other client applications as it can "talk" to any database via ODBC, ADO or native connection very easily. That sounds great! One easy-to-use tool versus several client softwares and, moreover, "with a lot of timesaving and useful features that can make your work with databases and an SQL code highly effective and comfortable". Is it all just a pie in the sky? - Well, let's learn more about Foxy SQL Pro features.

POWERSHELL SQL

Foxy SQL Pro allows you to:

* execute SQL commands and queries against any database,

* execute only chosen parts of an SQL script,

* create an Alias for often used connection parameters,

* browse data,

* define own types of comments, strings, terminators and keywords,

* record and save SQL scripts from and to a file,

POWERSHELL SQL

* save the result of the SQL command SELECT to a TXT, CSV or XML file,

* and much more.

Foxy SQL Pro Main Benefits:

* Direct support for at least six databases

(Interbase,Firebird, MySQL, Oracle, PostgeSQL, MS SQL Server etc.)

* One query tool versus a lof of client/server applications

* Available connections: ODBC, ADO, Native

POWERSHELL SQL

* User-friendly graphical Interface

* Wide range of useful and timesaving features

CHAPTER 19

ORACLE SQL CERTIFICATION: 1Z0-051 OR 1Z0-061?

The first of the Oracle 12c certification exams to go into production is 1Z0-061: Oracle Database 12c: SQL Fundamentals. Oracle University put this exam into production almost simultaneously with the retirement of the much older exam 1Z0-007: Introduction to Oracle9i SQL. However, the 11g version of the SQL Fundamentals exam, 1Z0-051, is still available. Having two equivalent exams in production leads to a fair amount of confusion among certification candidates. In this article I will discuss the two exams, what is different between them, and how to choose one over the other.

Either will satisfy the SQL requirement for the "Oracle Database 11g Administrator Certified Associate" or "Oracle PL/SQL

Developer Certified Associate" tracks. The SQL requirement can also be satisfied by passing 1Z0-047: Oracle Database SQL Expert. However, 1Z0-047 is a considerably harder exam than either 1Z0-051 or 1Z0-061. This is an option that should only be considered if you have worked with Oracle SQL extensively. This article focuses on the SQL fundamentals exams.

The 11g and 12c SQL Fundamentals exams are almost identical in terms of content covered and requirements satisfied for Oracle certifications. Oracle does not require you to use the 12c SQL Fundamentals when pursuing the 12c DBA track or the 11g exam for the DBA track in that release. Any Oracle SQL exam (including retired ones) can be used for any Oracle certification track that has a SQL requirement. For example, the SQL test I took over a decade ago was 1Z0-001: Introduction to Oracle: SQL and PL/SQL. That test has been retired for years, but could still be applied for the 12c track.

While the content of the two exams is very similar, there are a few differences. Both 1Z0-051 and 1Z0-061 contain forty-one topics. Of those, thirty-six are common to both exams. This means the tests have about 88% commonality by topic count. The last section of the 11g exam (Creating Other Schema Objects) was removed from the exam in the 12c version. The topics covered in that section are:

➢ Create simple and complex views
➢ Retrieve data from views
➢ Create, maintain, and use sequences
➢ Create and maintain indexes
➢ Create private and public synonyms

For the 1Z0-061 exam, Oracle University added a new 'Introduction' section with the following four topics:

➢ Describe the features of Oracle Database 12c
➢ Describe the salient features of Oracle Cloud 12c

> ➤ Explain the theoretical and physical aspects of a relational database
> ➤ Describe Oracle server's implementation of RDBMS and object relational database management system (ORDBMS)

They also added one more topic to the "Managing Tables using DML statements" section:

Truncate data

I have to say that I am very disappointed with Oracle University's decision to put TRUNCATE (which is a DDL operation) under a section specifically about DML statements. This is not something that makes sense in a test designed for people who are new to SQL. I am sure that OU would be heartbroken to learn of my disapproval.

The 1Z0-061 exam has nine more questions than 1Z0-051 (75 vs 66) and a slightly higher passing score (65% vs 60%). This does not necessarily mean that the test is harder to pass, though. The topics that have been added are ones that are likely to have questions that are more straightforward than the topics that were removed. OU has a certain target percentage of candidates that they want to pass each test on a first attempt. If they raised the passing score, it was because they felt the updated test had easier questions.

I have to say that choosing one test over the other is really a toss-up. The 11g exam is not particularly dated and all of the topics are still relevant. There might be a little bit of long-term benefit in having the 12c exam on your record rather than 11g, simply because 12c will be around after 11g is retired. However, 11g is currently the standard database used in production environments. Very few companies will have moved to 12c yet. In addition, none of my employers have inquired (or cared) about the specific tests I took to gain my Oracle certifications. Pick the exam that makes the most sense to you and you can be confident that you are not making a mistake. Whichever one you choose, good luck on the test.

CHAPTER 20

STUDY GUIDE FOR 1Z0-061:
ORACLE DATABASE 12C:
SQL FUNDAMENTALS

Several Oracle certification tracks, including the Database Administrator OCA and Database Developer OCA, require that candidates pass a SQL certification exam. At this time, 1Z0-061 is one of three exams currently being offered that fulfil the SQL requirement. There are two other current exams, 1Z0-051 and 1Z0-047, as well as two retired exams: 1Z0-001 and 1Z0-007 that will fulfil the SQL requirement. Retired exams can no longer be scheduled, but if you passed these before they were retired, Oracle Education will still accept them as your SQL requirement.

In addition to the certification requirement, SQL knowledge is an extremely important aspect of working with the Oracle database. If you are new to the Oracle database, this exam makes a really good entry point into the certification process as the SQL Fundamentals exam is one of the least difficult Oracle certification tests that you will experience. This is not to say that the test is not a pushover -- taking it without being prepared is likely to result in failure. This chapter is intended to provide some insight to assist in your efforts to study for the exam.

The Oracle Education website lists all of the topics that will be covered in the 1Z0-061 exam. There are significant commands and capabilities in Oracle SQL that are not listed there. However, no test questions will deal with material outside of that list. The topics that Oracle Education provides for each exam are always complete. The 12c SQL Fundamentals exam has forty-one topics in ten subject areas. The test itself will have seventy-five multiple-choice or multiple-answer questions and you'll have two hours to complete it. The passing score is sixty-five percent. For the multiple-answer questions, there is no partial credit. Any questions that are left unanswered will count as incorrect. You should never leave any exam question unanswered -- even if that means that you must pick one of the choices at random.

The majority of the exam questions will have one or more SQL statements involved -- either as part of the question or as answer choices. You must be able to differentiate between functional and non-functional SQL without having an Oracle instance to execute them on. Often one or more of the SQL statements among the answers will have a flaw that would cause them to generate an error if executed. If you are able to recognize this and eliminate them, determining the correct answer is easier. Because this is Oracle's SQL Fundamentals exam, the vast majority of the SQL statements presented will be both straightforward and relatively small. You will have to understand how to use several common SQL functions. While most of the test is about DML statements, you must understand the DDL syntax to create several common database object types. Most of the functionality covered by this exam involves common SQL tasks that database developers or administrators are likely to use reasonably often.

Many of the questions on this exam will have exhibits associated with them. The exhibits often contain a SQL statement or a set of tables that a SQL statement is operating against. They are intended to provide information that may help you to answer the question. Viewing these exhibits takes time and not every one is really required in order to answer the question. The test interface will specifically state that you should view the exhibit and then answer the question. I recommend that you read the question and answers and then view the exhibit. Sometimes you will find that you can skip viewing the exhibit entirely. Even if you do need it, looking at the question and answers first will give you an idea of specifically what to look for when you view the exhibit. Either outcome will save you some time.

CHAPTER 21

HOW TO RESET SA PASSWORD IN SQL SERVER 2000

Microsoft SQL Server 2000 is a full-featured relational database management system that offers a variety of administrative tools to ease the burdens of database development, maintenance and administration. It operates in one of two authentication modes: Windows Authentication Mode (the default) or Mixed Mode.

When you install the SQL Server 2000, you can log in the server with Windows Authentication and SQL Server Authentication if you select mixed mode authentication. If you select Windows Authentication, you cannot assign a SA password during installation. However, you should set the password after installation.

It is very easy for one to set SA password in SQL 2000. Just follow the below steps:

* 1. Expand a server group, and then expand a server.

* 2. Expand Security, and then click Logins.

* 3. In the details pane, right-click SA, and then click Properties.

* 4. In the Password box, type the new password.

The type of client connections determines the choice of security mode. If all of the incoming clients support trusted connections, you can use Windows Authentication Mode. If some clients do not support trusted connections, you can select Mixed Mode.

If you forget the SA password, you will need to use MS SQL Server Password Unlocker to reset the password for SQL 2000. MS SQL Server Password Unlocker is easy yet powerful SQL password reset software for you to reset SQL password, including reset SA password and other user passwords. It provides you an easy and safe way to reset SQL password for Microsoft SQL Server 2000/2005/2008 in a minute. No need for you to reinstall SQL on your PC. The file in master.mdf format is enough for you to recover SA password SQL 2000.

Steps to reset SQL 2000 password for SA as follows:

* 1. Download and install MS SQL Server Password Unlocker.

* 2. Click the application icon to run it.

* 3. Click Open to import your master.mdf file. All the user names of your MS SQL will be displayed.

* 4. Select SA account, click Change password button to reset the password.

* 5. Type a new password, and then click OK to finish your operation.

PL-SQL INSTRUCTIONS

PL/SQL is Oracle's Procedure language or programming language. It is very similar to other programming languages. We can record specific instructions in PL/SQL that tell our applications how to act. PL/SQL has a wealth of tools that greatly enhance the processing of records. PL/SQL has looping statements that enable you to perform the same function a number of times.

It has condition logic that enables you to process records when certain conditions are met. It has cursors that enable you to move sets of records into memory and process them one at a time. PL/SQL code is grouped into structures called blocks. If you create a stored procedure or package,you give the block of PL/SQL code a name; if the block of PL/SQL code is not given a name, then it is said to be an anonymous block. The examples in this chapter will feature anonymous blocks of PL/SQL code; the following chapters in this section illustrate the creation of named blocks.

The main difference between SQL and PL/SQL is, In SQL's we can give one SQl command at a time but using PL/SQL we can give more than one SQL command at a time. Within a PL/SQL block, the first section is the Declarations section. Inside the Declarations section, you define the variables and cursors that the block will use.

The Declarations section starts with the keyword declare and ends when the Executable Commands section starts (as indicated by "begin"). The Executable Commands section is followed by the Exception Handling section; the exception keyword signals the start of the Exception Handling section. The PL/SQL block is terminated by the end keyword.

The structure of a typical PL/SQL block is shown in the following listing:

Declaration Part.

The declarative section such as variable declarations, cursor declarations etc.

Execution Part.

POWERSHELL SQL

The Executable section. The complete programming codes are in this section.

Exception part

The exception handling section. If any error raised in the execution part, the controls just skip to the exception handling part. (Here the Declarative section and Exception handling section are optional. But the Execution section is must).

Declare

The Declarative Statements.

Begin

The Statements for execution.

Exception

The Error Handling Part

End;

Declarations Section

The Declarations section begins a PL/SQL block. The Declarations section starts with the declare keyword, followed by a list of variable and cursor definitions.

Executable Commands Section

In the Executable Commands section, you manipulate the variables and cursors declared in the Declarations section of your

PL/SQL block. The Executable Commands section always starts with the keyword begin.

Exception Handling Section

When user-defined or system-related exceptions (errors) are encountered, the control of the PL/SQL block shifts to the Exception Handling section. Within the Exception Handling section, the when clause is used to evaluate which exception is to be "raised"-that is, executed.

CHAPTER 22

VMWARE VCENTER AND MICROSOFT SQL SERVER REPORTING SERVICES

I know this might be a weird combination, but if you ever have to install VMWare vCenter 4.0 and MS SQL including Reporting Service on the same machine (Windows Server 2008 64 Bit), this is how it is done. Be warned, VMWare will eventually not support this configuration, but I had no issues with that up to this point.

VMWare vCenter requires a SQL database (SQL 2005 or SQL 2008 at the time of this writing). While you can use a remote database we had the need for a local installation as well as we needed SQL Server Reporting service installed. After installing the Windows Operating System we did a full install of SQL Server 2005 including SP3. We did try this with SQL 2008 before, but SQL 2008 is no longer using IIS to manage the Reporting Services and that made it very difficult to manage the 2 applictions and their ports that they use (hint: overlapping ports are 80 and 443).

After you installed SQL 2005, you can install vSphere vCenter 4. During the installation you can change the ports that vCenter uses, however this does not work. SQL Report Services needs port 443 for internal communication. I had changed the port in vCenter to 444 when using SQL 2008, but apparently vCenter ignores that port setting and still locks port 443 later one - making Reporting Services kaput. So, install vCenter with the default ports.

Now go into IIS (hint: SQL 2005 requires that you install ALL IIS items in Server 2008) and change the port for the reporting services to port 81. There is no need to touch port 443 to get MS SQL Reporting Services to work. Now open up the Report Services Configuration tool and select the Web Service Identity tab. Set the appPool to "Classic.NET" for the Report Server and the Report Manager.

MS SQL Reporting services should work just fine as long as you specify the new port in the URL when accessing the reports.

Why did SQL 2008 not work for me? SQL 2008 Report Services does use HTTPS traffic much more than SQL 2005 does. Since VMWare vcenter locks that port (even if you tell it not to), SQL 2008 Reporting Services will not function properly. Please note that this is a very high level view at the problems related to running VMWare vCenter and MS SQL Reporting Services from the same server.

CONCLUSION

Microsoft's new attitude towards security: "We will rethink our approach to security. We will examine our code for vulnerabilities. We will release patches as needed. We will turn off most features by default in order to keep the footprint small. If you need something, turn it on. But if you don't need it, leave it off. That way if a vulnerability is discovered in a product you are not using, you won't be affected."

Some people claim that a big security hole in SQL Server 2000 was the ability to issue command shell commands using xp_cmdshell. I would argue that the most of the blatant security "holes" were a result of a combination of poor design and human error. Specifically:

a) the default password for the system administrator account (sa) was blank

b) the service account that SQL Server was configured to use was far too often a domain administrator account thus escalating the privileges of any account that used xp_cmdshell

c) Microsoft failed to detect vulnerabilities in their source code and took too long to release patches once the vulnerabilities were identified

d) DBA's failed to keep the latest patches applied thus leaving their servers vulnerable to known exploits

A good case study regarding SQL 2000's vulnerabilities is the Sasser virus (early 2001 I believe). This virus spread rapidly by searching out unpatched SQL Server's. There were an unbelievable amount of these servers exposed on the internet, including SQL Server's run by financial institutions. Sasser did a lot of damage. Sasser did this by executing remote procedure calls on unpatched servers. You could say that running remote procedure calls should be turned off, but then you would be effectively be eliminating the whole "Client/Server" approach from modern day computing.

The solution to Sasser style attacks is of course is two-fold. Microsoft must be determined to hunt down vulnerabilities in their code and release patches in a timely fashion, and we as DBA's must be vigilant in applying those patches.

When it comes to SQL 20005 and features like xp_cmdshell, we have to remember that Microsoft built these features to allow database developer to develop rich applications capable of performing complex processing tasks. It is NOT Microsoft's intention that people keep these features turned off . Rather, the administrator (DBA) has to make the effort to turn the features on if they are required. Keep your application footprint small and reduce your exposure to attack.

You could say that the most secure SQL Server is one that is turned off. That would not be very useful to anyone, and somebody could still walk away with a backup of the database. They could even simply yank out the hard drives and put them in bag like yesterday's dirty tupperware.

File System Objects (FSO) in my opinion is a great alternative to using the xp_cmdshell if all you are doing is manipulating files. Microsoft created FSO so ALL its scripting languages (C#, Visual Basic, T-SQL, etc) can have access to file system objects without having the ability to execute arbitrary commands.

Here are some other features that are turned off by default:

> openrowset / opendatasource Allows SQL Server to query an outside datasource without having to define a "linked server"
> CLR - Common Runtime Language This is one of the biggest selling features for SQL 2005 which allows you to code SQL procedures that include code from any of the .NET applications

Database Mail Allows the database processes to send email messages via SMTP

As I have already stated, these features are only turned off to minimize the footprint of the SQL Server. The smaller the footprint, the less code that is running that may be vulnerable to attack. The features are neither bad nor insecure. But if you don't need them, don't' run them.

Other features

Bulk Insert is an example of a feature that is not "turned off" by default, but you need special permission to use. User accounts that wish to perform bulk inserts must first be assigned the role of "BulkAdmin".

You must also be aware of how SQL 2005 handles security when bulk inserting data. In 2000, the account that the SQL Server service account used had to have permission to access the file. In SQL Server 2005, the user issuing the command must have access to the file.

We experienced a very frustrating and difficult to solve problem when we tried to perform bulk inserts across a network.

The problem that we encountered is that the current network configuration is not

POWERSHELL SQL

"Kerberos Protocol 5" compliant, which prevents SQL Server from passing on the credentials of the logged in user. This is more commonly referred to as the "Two Network Hop" problem. We log in to SQL to issue a command (hop 1). SQL tries to grab the file from a network share using our credentials (hop 2). The primary domain controller responds saying "I don't know what you are trying to do".

The LAN administration team who was helping us solve the problem were perplexed as to why we were having difficulty, when they were not. I solved that mystery when I realized that the LAN administrators were using remote desktop to connect to the server then they would open Management Studio directly on the server to issue the Bulk insert command. For all intents and purposes they were logging into the SQL Server locally (no network hop involved). SQL Server was able to grab the file across the network because only one network hop was involved.

REFERENCES

"Release v6.2.2 Release of PowerShell Core". GitHub PowerShell Core repository. Retrieved 2019-07-18.

"Release v7.0.0-preview.2 Release of PowerShell". GitHub PowerShell Core repository. Retrieved 2019-07-18.

"PowerShell for every system!". 12 June 2017 – via GitHub.

Snover, Jeffrey (May 25, 2008). "PowerShell and WPF: WTF". Windows PowerShell Blog. Microsoft.

Bright, Peter (18 August 2016). "PowerShell is Microsoft's latest open source release, coming to Linux, OS X". Ars Technica. Condé Nast.

"How Windows PowerShell works". Microsoft Developer Network. Microsoft. Retrieved 2007-11-27.

Truher, Jim (December 2007). "Extend Windows PowerShell With Custom

Commands". MSDN Magazine. Microsoft. Archived from the original on 6 October 2008.

Lowe, Scott (January 4, 2007). "Exchange 2007: Get used to the command line". TechRepublic. CBS Interactive.

Snover, Jeffrey (November 13, 2007). "SQL Server Support for PowerShell!". Windows PowerShell Blog (blog posting). Microsoft.

Dragan, Richard V. (April 23, 2003). "Windows Server 2003 Delivers Improvements All Around". Reviews. PC Magazine. Ziff Davis. A standout feature here is that virtually all admin utilities now work from the command line (and most are available through telnet).

Biggar and Harbaugh (2017-09-14). "The Man Behind Windows PowerShell". To Be Continuous (Podcast). Heavybit. Retrieved 2017-09-14.

Snover, Jeffrey (August 2, 2002). "Monad Manifesto – the Origin of Windows

PowerShell". Windows PowerShell Blog (blog posting). Microsoft.

"Windows PowerShell (Monad) Has Arrived". Windows PowerShell Blog. Microsoft. April 25, 2006.

Snover, Jeffrey (November 15, 2006). "Windows PowerShell & Windows Vista". Windows PowerShell Blog (blog posting). Microsoft.

"Windows Management Framework (Windows PowerShell 2.0, WinRM 2.0, and BITS 4.0)". Support. Microsoft. September 30, 2013. Archived from the original on October 13, 2013.

"What is Pester and Why Should I Care?".

Snover, Jeffrey (18 August 2016). "PowerShell is open sourced and is available on Linux". Microsoft Azure Blog. Microsoft.

POWERSHELL SQL

Do not go yet; One last thing to do

If you enjoyed this book or found it useful I'd be very grateful if you'd post a short review on it. Your support really does make a difference and I read all the reviews personally so I can get your feedback and make this book even better.

Thanks again for your support!